THE EVANGELICAL ROOTS OF DEMOCRACY

"Where there is no vision, the people perish."
Proverbs 29:18

THOMAS L. MAMMOSER

ISBN: 1493517430
ISBN 13: 9781493517435
Library of Congress Control Number: 2014902764
CreateSpace Independent Publishing Platform
North Charleston, South Carolina

Contents

Chapter One: Introduction

"Intelligence, patriotism, Christianity, and a firm reliance on Him, who has never forsaken this favored land, are still competent to adjust, in the best way, all our present difficulty."

A braham Lincoln spoke these words just weeks before the outbreak of the Civil War, the most extreme torment this country ever experienced.[1]

The greatness of Lincoln was in standing up for a principle—and for a vulnerable and suffering people —in spite of enormous pressures for 'expediency' and facing a tragic war that would kill many thousands of his beloved citizens.

The principle he defended was that all men are created equal and that they must be treated justly and with dignity. This, of course, included those most defenseless at the time, enslaved black people. At the time of Lincoln's second inaugural, approximately one-eighth of the U.S. population was in slavery.

Lincoln issued the Emancipation Proclamation, freeing all slaves in the Confederate territory, on January 1, 1863. Today, in the Fisk University Library in Nashville, one can find a copy of the Bible inscribed as follows: "To Abraham Lincoln, President of the United States, the Friend of Universal Freedom, from the Loyal Colored People of Baltimore, as a token of respect and Gratitude. Baltimore, 4th July 1864."

Greatly supported by Lincoln, the Thirteenth Amendment made slavery illegal everywhere in the United States, effective in December, 1865.

Lincoln's response to the colored people of Baltimore showed his respect for the Holy Scriptures. "In regard to this Great book," he replied, "I have but to say, it is the best gift God has given to man." Then, to make his meaning even clearer, he concluded, "All the good Savior gave to the world was communicated through this book. But for it we could not know right from wrong. All things most desirable for man's welfare, here and hereafter, are to be found portrayed in it." [2]

We are at a difficult juncture in our nation, when another fundamental freedom— freedom of conscience— is not only not being defended but called into question. And so it seems imperative today to look to our past and attempt to rediscover the foundational wisdom, the governing principles, and, yes, the religious roots upon which this unique nation —the world's beacon of democracy —was built.

It is a precious wisdom and they are profound roots. And they are in jeopardy today to a religious dismissiveness, a moral relativism, an intellectual subjectivism and an historical obtuseness —not to mention a bourgeois liberalism anxious to make everyone a little god —that appears eager to deconstruct our past and ignore the faith and wisdom of the Founders. Men who understood that "the laws of nature and nature's God," as the Declaration of Independence put it, was an interdependence that made our country a special, "favored land" of high moral purpose.

Democracy and Religion: Separate... or Distinct

These laws were meant to be distinguished—give to God's what is God's and to Caesar what is Caesar's —because they are distinct. Unlike Church and state, however, they were not meant to be separated. At the level of daily life, as the Founders clearly saw and encouraged, they are meant to be deeply joined. Joined because, as they said over and over, one flows from the other. The law of nature—the natural law that presents itself to every man's conscience and is meant to guide his behavior—flows from the law of God ... the author of Lincoln's great Book. Indeed conscience is man's foremost *quid divinum*.

In any distinction, of course, there is an order of values. And if the things of God are distinct from those that are Caesar's, it does not mean they are separate. It means they occupy a higher place. They are essentially spiritual ... they are linked to eternity and, properly understood, capable of making man God-like. But they in no way threaten the kingdoms of this earth. In the traditional terms of St. Thomas Aquinas (1225-1274), it could be said quite simply: Grace—God's action—perfects nature, it does not destroy it.

Indeed the task of religion is to help guide, enlighten and vivify these kingdoms because its adherents are at the same time society's members. Their wellbeing requires a necessary cooperation between the Church and the body politic. The Church may be a 'stranger and an exile', exhorting its members to resist the natural appetites which besiege the soul. It is not an enemy; indeed, it is meant to be an instrument of grace in creating the 'city upon a hill'[3] that Puritan John Winthrop foresaw nearly 400 years ago.

The most relevant example of 'distinct but not separate' from the Judeo-Christian culture of the Founders is in the great commandments: love of God, love of neighbor. They are presented, both in Deuteronomy and in the New Testament, as being two distinct forms of love ultimately meant to be united. We separate and ignore these laws— and these commandments— at our peril.

Hopefully we Americans realize we are at a challenging moment in our history, when our distinctively religious foundation is being threatened as never before —by a confused and confusing culture, to be sure,— but also by a freely elected government. Catholics, Christians— people of all faiths— should feel pressured by and want to defend against a government that demands the violation of such a basic liberty, that of conscience itself.

As the conflict of values rages over the administration's health-care mandate and other issues, it seems imperative to reflect on the larger relationship between democracy and religion in America and its historical roots, lest we forget our very identity as a people. Who we are, what we stand for, and most importantly, *where we are going.*

Freedom and Christianity

Rev. Martin Luther King, Jr., in his famous "Letter from Birmingham Jail" in 1963, reminded us that: "The goal of America is freedom" and argued that making America fully aware of that goal was a specific obligation of Christians.

As King wrote, "I would agree with Saint Augustine, that 'an unjust law is no law at all.' Now what is the difference between the two? How does one determine when a law is just or unjust? A just law is a man-made code that squares with the moral law or the law of God. An unjust law is a code that is out of harmony with the moral law. To put it in the terms of Saint Thomas Aquinas, an unjust law is a human law that is not rooted in eternal law and natural law."[4]

Thomas Jefferson said it this way: "No provision in our Constitution ought to be dearer to man than that which protects the rights of conscience against the power of its public functionaries, were it possible that any of these should consider a conquest over the conscience of men either attainable or applicable to any desirable purpose."[5]

Americans hopefully know that, but maybe not. We are a long way from our founding, with countless modern distractions. But we should know that, and we should want to protect such a beneficent culture. We should also feel threatened by the current state of affairs because it is not only religion—our first freedom—that is at stake, but also an authentically human and intelligent approach to government.

An approach that is firmly grounded, not only on our unique religious history, but on rationality, reason and—yes— grace. Where it appears to be tending, unfortunately, is toward relativism, agnosticism, whim and a Nietzscheian 'will to power.'

More than 150 years ago Alexis de Tocqueville wrote: "There is no country in the whole world in which the Christian religion retains a greater influence over the souls of men than in America. Religion is the foremost of the institutions of the country." As he wrote in *Democracy in America*: "In France I had almost always seen the spirit of religion and the spirit of freedom pursuing courses diametrically opposed to each other; but in America I found that they were intimately united, and that they reigned in common over the same country."[6]

The Reverend Louis Dwight (1793-1854), a Yale graduate noted for his prison work, once wrote to Tocqueville that the Americans were the best-educated people on earth. "(Here) everyone takes for granted that education will be moral and religious. There would be a general outcry, a kind of popular uprising, against anyone who tried to introduce a contrary system, and everyone would say it would be better to have no education at all than an education of that sort. It is from the Bible that all our children learn to read."[7]

We do well to ask ourselves: Would Tocqueville even recognize today the country he thought so special?

Tocqueville was also to affirm that "the advent of Jesus Christ upon earth was required to teach that all members of the human race are by nature equal and the like."[8] Twenty years earlier Hegel had expressed a similar view: "It is fully fifteen hundred years since through the influence of Christianity the freedom of the person began to flourish, and at least in a small section of the human race takes rank as a universal principle." [9]

The Meaning of Religion

It's inspiring, in our secularized times, to reflect on how very seriously the Founders of our country took the notion of religious truth and "the advent of Jesus Christ upon earth."[10] They did so not only because many were fervent believers —faith was integral to their history and identity —but also because it spoke to a unique destiny they saw for America. They believed a culturally religious country was necessary; only such a county could foster virtue and give the fledgling democracy coherence. Religion helped unite and inspire America. It made it extraordinary; they could hardly envision a secular *res publica*.

But what do we mean here by 'religion' and a 'religious culture'? 'Religion' — the Latin *'religio'*—at its root doesn't refer to denomination or creed but to what is sacred. At its core religion means respect for what is holy, i.e., the practice of faith and the service and worship of God. *Religio,* and its Latin derivatives *religiose* and *religiosus,* all refer to doing things with rectitude, i.e., with conscience. This meant a great deal to the Founders. Whatever their respective beliefs, they could also not envision an 'unvirtuous' republic. Nor, for that matter, an attenuated conscience.

Insofar as freedom of conscience is involved, then, in a primary way what we mean here is not religion as denomination or creed but religion as practiced. Religion—in the most profound sense –as *inspiration*. We are referring to the exercise of a personal freedom, with the right to worship collectively as well as personally according to one's conscience.

This distinction is critical. It is religion as *denomination*—a specific belief or creed— that was wisely forbidden establishment by our founding fathers. And, it bears saying, which has permitted freedom of worship for all citizens and helped them distinguish that which is Caesar's from that which is God's.

It is religion in the sense of personal service and worship that is specifically protected by the Constitution *in its exercise*— a protection which has always been recognized —by position in the text and by language—as more exalted than the mere ban on the abridgment of free speech. Public profession of beliefs and creeds are provided for separately in the second clause of the First Amendment, through forbidding Congress from making any law "abridging the freedom of speech or of the press."

The argument proposed here is that, whatever the individualism of the Founders or, for that matter, of contemporary culture, man is by nature social—he is in *communio* with others. Therefore it is only a practiced, personal religion that is authentic — (i.e., reflective of its Trinitarian author and thus, in philosophical terms, 'naturally diffusive' and overflowing) — that can possibly lead to a higher culture. That is to say a faith-inspired culture that is respectful of the beliefs and consciences of all citizens—indeed *loves* all citizens— and is capable of promoting a better life for each of them.

Further Distinctions

Our Founders also had an instinctive respect for religion as denomination, as we will see. They firmly believed the future of the nation was linked to recognizing the importance of faith in God and its encouragement by religious creeds. They wanted to *protect* these creeds, they just did not want to *establish* them. Peter Drucker provides some clarity as to the spiritual/theocentric dimensions of creed, which is important in distinguishing creed from ideology, and, indeed, religion from secular belief.

"Religion today as in 1790," Drucker writes, "clearly means two things. To be a 'religion', a creed must be supernatural. It must be based on an acknowledgement of a power above man — Jefferson's 'common father and creator of man'. To be a religion a creed must be based on divine reason and divine will rather than solely upon natural reason. It must find its sanction not in the human mind, not in morality and ethics, but in an appeal to the supernatural. Otherwise, as the Conscientious Objectors' decisions of the Supreme Court reiterated, it is not a religion but an ideology."[11]

> Regarding conscientious objection Chief Justice Hughes, in his opinion in *United States v. Macintosh*, (1931), enunciated the rationale behind the long recognition of conscientious objection to participation in war accorded by Congress in our various conscription laws when he declared that, "in the forum of conscience, duty to a moral power higher than the state has always been maintained."

> In a similar vein, Harlan Fiske Stone, later Chief Justice, drew from the nation's past when he declared that "both morals and sound policy require that the state should not violate the conscience of the individual. All our history gives confirmation to the view that liberty of conscience has a moral and social value which makes it worthy of preservation at the hands of the state."

> Stone continued, "So deep in its significance and vital, indeed, is it to the integrity of man's moral and spiritual nature that nothing short of the self-preservation of the state should warrant its violation; and it may well be questioned whether the state which preserves its life by a settled policy of violation of the conscience of the individual will not in fact ultimately lose it by the process." [12]

Secondly, Drucker distinguishes religion from ideology. He writes: "a religion must seek its kingdom in the other world. A creed, however infallible it claims to be, is not a religion—as the Constitution and the American tradition understand the term—if it aims at establishing its kingdom in this world. This also means, however, that religion must acknowledge the existence of a 'kingdom of this world,' that is, of an autonomous realm of natural reason, an expression of which is the Constitution and the allegiance of American citizenship. It need not approve of this world."[13]

By 'religion' then our Founders meant two distinct things, one denominational and the other personal. In the establishment clause prohibiting "an establishment of religion" they obviously meant 'denomination', the choice of which government had no right to mandate for the country. Whereas in the 'free exercise' clause they are, just as obviously, protecting the personal practice *of* religion— freedom of conscience — which may, of course, have collective ramifications since virtually all religions have a social dimension.

So by religion here —and in arguing for the evangelically grounded democratic tenets that protect it — we are not concerned primarily with religion as 'denominational', i.e., as an established creed. What we are concerned with is what the founding fathers meant in the 'free exercise' clause. Namely a personal (necessarily involving conscience) and, therefore, a 'theocentric' activity of the human person that acknowledges God and is oriented to God.

This orientation distinguishes it from that which is anthropocentric or man-centered. For example, an ideology, which operates on a horizontal plane and is centered fundamentally, if not exclusively, on men and women as a collectivity of individuals. That is, as citizens, party members, workers —but not as unique persons, each with a divine calling and destiny. This is a crucial distinction, especially as we are dealing here precisely with the denial of man's most intimate and most human freedom and which defines his personhood. Namely his inner, theocentric freedom— his conscience.

We will further argue that this theocentric activity of the human person — specifically as it relates to belief in the God of Christianity as demonstrated in both the religious beliefs and reasoned convictions of our Founders—has been the driving force and intellectual underpinning of American democracy from its inception. A democracy much threatened today by a collective amnesia that is forgetting its most fundamental roots.

Historical Amnesia

Nations are like persons in that they have a defining history (one might say a 'mind and memory') that they ignore at their peril. Because, dormant in this memory—in our case this Christian tradition—is what made this nation what it is and, as importantly, is the seed of what it might become. Europe and America, both suffering their own forms of historical amnesia, appear badly in need of a sense of mission these days. 'Freedom,' 'hope' and 'change,' indeed. But for what?

To be sure, nations, like persons, need homes, jobs, education, peace and security. To achieve their full stature, however, they also need soul, meaning, authentic hope and direction. Better put, perhaps, they need a sense of where they are going, and of what they could become.

This 'mind and memory' is not only a shaper of a nation's present. Its higher values— justly recognized —can also be a guide for their future, which needs the dynamic of intelligibility and serious purpose to energize it forward. A future, we would argue, that must draw life not merely from the wooly language of promise, change and toleration but from a renewed and robust engagement —of both mind *and* heart— with the great metaphysical strengths of the Western tradition and with its guiding spiritual force—Christianity.

This is not the whole story, to be sure. But this is needed in America today, at least in part, because of a culturally deficient awareness of our nation's heritage. As when President Obama declared during his April 2009 visit to Turkey that "one of the great strengths of the United States is ... we do not consider ourselves a Christian nation or a Jewish nation or a Muslim nation. We consider ourselves a nation of citizens who are bound by ideals and a set of values."[14]

President Obama is right; America is not a denominationally Christian nation. This was, in many ways, *the* issue for the Founders, and their response was quite clear and unambiguous. But so also was their intent to support —we might even say *enshrine*—a set of ideals and values into the fabric of our founding documents, convinced they were indispensable to this nation's future. And the religion to which they looked for inspiration in protecting these values is indisputable.

So we can say: Of course we are bound by 'ideals and values'. The question is: What are they and where do they come from? Are they still binding—and do they have religious roots? It would certainly seem so, as this book attempts to demonstrate. As recently as thirty years ago these roots were still publicly visible when our government officially dedicated an entire year to celebrating the Bible. The action was taken at the behest of a national committee consisting of 85 percent of our nation's top religious leaders, representing the Catholic, Jewish and Protestant faiths.

The ninety-seventh Congress declared the Bible "The Word of God" under Public Law 97—280 on October 4, 1982. That month President Reagan signed into law the *1983 Year of the Bible Proclamation*. Scores of governors and mayors that year were to sign their own "1983 Year of the Bible Proclamations," and millions of Bibles were distributed and read nationwide that year.

Some opening sentences of the bill reflect its message and tone:

> "Whereas Biblical teachings inspired concepts of civil government that are contained in our Declaration of Independence and the Constitution of the United States;
>
> Whereas this Nation now faces great challenges that will test this Nation as it has never been tested before; and
>
> Whereas that renewing our knowledge of and faith in God through Holy Scripture can strengthen us as a nation and a people ..."[15]

Thirty years later, a similar proclamation was proposed in the 111th Congress, encouraging President Obama to designate 2010 "The National Year of the Bible." It didn't happen. None of the many Christian Democrats in Congress signed on as co-sponsors. So much for Abraham Lincoln's 'greatest Gift'. The opening lines of the 2010 proclamation are nonetheless historically honest and instructive:

"Whereas the Bible has had a profound impact in shaping America into a great Nation;

> Whereas deep religious beliefs stemming from the Old and New Testament of the Bible have inspired Americans from all walks of life especially the early settlers, whose faith, spiritual courage, and moral strength enabled them to endure intense hardships in this new land;
>
> Whereas many of our Presidents have recognized the importance of God and the Bible ..."[16]

In fairness to President Obama, he used two Bibles at his inauguration, one the Bible Abraham Lincoln used in 1861 in his first inaugural ceremony, as well as a 'traveling Bible' used by the Rev. Martin Luther King, Jr. One commentator read this selection "as the president's assent to a theological tradition that runs from the Puritans to Lincoln to King and beyond."[17] The assent is often difficult to determine. But the tradition is ours, it is special, and its recognition is welcome in this high venue.

But the question remains: Do our leaders generally— and as importantly our citizenry— really know and embrace this theological tradition anymore? Does our tradition yet guide us in our public affairs, not just in governmental decision-making but in the ambience of everyday life? It would seem foolishly naive to be affirmative on that score these days. More likely we might share the view that "we are all immigrants today, living in a culture whose stories are not our stories and whose values are not our values."[18]

As for inaugural history, God is mentioned or referred to in all inaugural addresses except Washington's second, which is a very brief (two paragraphs) and perfunctory acknowledgement. In his first inaugural, Washington refers to God as "that Almighty Being who rules the universe," "Great Author of every public and private good," "Invisible Hand," and "benign Parent of the Human Race." John Adams refers to God as "Providence," "Being who is supreme over all," "Patron of Order," "Fountain of Justice," and "Protector in all ages of the world of virtuous liberty".

Jefferson speaks of "that Infinite Power which rules the destinies of the universe," and "that Being in whose hands we are." Madison speaks of "that Almighty Being whose power regulates the destiny of nations," and "Heaven." Monroe uses "Providence" and "the Almighty" in his first inaugural and "Almighty God" in his second.[19]

The fact remains that it is all too easy to forget, and, evidently, to *want* to forget. Which is why each generation needs raise the question: What historic values really do bind us together as a nation? What ideals gave birth to the unique American experiment, and where do these ideals and values originate? Religious conscience protection—so fundamental to our way of life— has been a part of the American experiment for nearly four centuries. Where did it come from? Better yet, is it still operative?

It appears highly vulnerable today. While the ambiguous totems of equality, tolerance, choice, etc. fly high, the religion that engendered these values—and most importantly with the potency to guide us to a better future —is under overt attack. For we argue here that it is the Judeo/Christian religion that nurtured this nation and helped our Founders articulate its God-given, inalienable rights. A reinvigoration of this faith, not its abandonment, is needed to sustain our guiding principles of nationhood and protect the hinge of all our freedoms, that of freedom of conscience.

There is much to fear for all Christians, indeed for all people of good will, from not knowing the "ideals and values" question. Ignorance of our history and our identity as a nation—undeniably Christian in inspiration —threatens freedom and democracy at home and across the globe. Indeed all religious people need awaken to an "aggressive secularism"—one might call it a cultural agnosticism— that "is beginning to turn into an ideology that imposes itself through politics and leaves no space for the Catholic and Christian vision."[20]

Chapter Two: A (Bit of) American History

"It is one thing to say that Columbus discovered America. It is something else to realize that he opened the door to the most phenomenal spread of Christianity since the time of St. Paul." [21]

It would be fair to say that America's remarkable religious history had a notable prehistory as well, suggesting an almost mystical future that began with its legendary discoverer, Christopher Columbus.

Christopher Columbus (1451-1506), a native of Genoa, a great adventurer and an ardent Catholic, was seeking a new route to India, convinced that by sailing west he could reach Asia. Having been declined financial help in Portugal for his daring vision, the friars of La Rabida in Seville, teachers of his son Diego, helped him approach Queen Isabella of Spain for help.

After much delay, her royal treasurer, Luis de Santangel, entered the debate, arguing that the expedition "could provide so great service to God and the exaltation of his Church" that to decline the option would be "a grave reproach" to that divine order.[22]

Queen Isabella commissioned her "Admiral of the Ocean Sea" on April 30, 1492 with this exhortation: "Whereas you, Christobal Colon, are setting forth by our command ... to discover and acquire certain islands and mainlands in the ocean sea ... it is our will and pleasure that you shall discover and acquire the same for the glory of God and the wealth of God's great nation, Spain."[23]

Whatever its commercial and political ramifications, there is little question Columbus was embarking on a religious mission. His lead ship was the *Santa Maria,* and the island he discovered, after thirty-three days of sailing, was named *San Salvador,* Holy Savior. His journey's first diary entry expressed the hope he could make contact with the native peoples to find out "the manner in which may be undertaken their conversion to our Holy Faith."

On November 27, 1492, he wrote " ... and I say that your Highness ought not to consent to any foreigner does business or sets foot here, except Christian Catholics, since it is the end and the beginning of the enterprise, that it should be for the enhancement and glory of the Christian religion ... "[24]

King Ferdinand and Queen Isabella granted Columbus's request for a second voyage, charging the Admiral Viceroy and Governor "that by all ways and means he strive and endeavor to win over the inhabitants of the said Islands and Mainland to be converted to our Holy Catholic Faith," and that all who sail with him "treat the said Indians very well and lovingly and abstain from doing them any injury, arranging that both people hold much conversation and intimacy, each serving the others to the best of their ability."

They added: "Priests and clerics will be sent to see that they be carefully taught the principles of Our Holy Faith ... and if some person or persons should maltreat the said Indians in any manner whatsoever, the said Admiral ... shall punish them severely..." Columbus's second voyage in the fall of 1493, described by one author as "magnificent," involved seventeen ships and some 1,200 men, including friars. [25]

Columbus was a regular communicant, given to daily prayer. He was also a great lover of books; his reading included a wide range of classical, scientific and theological authors, including Flavius Josephus, St. Augustine, St. Thomas Aquinas and St. John Chrysostom. Columbus was an assiduous student of religious writings—especially the Bible, to which he was devoted. And he was also an author; his *Book of Prophecies*, while virtually unknown in America, reveals the remarkable influence Holy Scripture had on his vision of discovery and evangelization.[26]

His son Ferdinand wrote of him, "He was so strict in matters of religion that for fasting and saying prayers he might have been taken for a member of a religious order." Columbus interpreted his expedition in scriptural terms, as when he wrote in 1493 that his success was due not to his own merit "but to the holy Christian faith, and to the piety and religion of our Sovereigns."[27]

And he added, "Let Christ rejoice on earth, as he rejoices in heaven in the prospect of the salvation of the souls of so many nations hitherto lost." As the authors of *The Religious History of America* point out, "the discovery of America was the climax of a great pilgrimage, the end of a noble spiritual quest as well as the opening of (a) new millennial epoch in salvation history."[28]

Colonization and Religion

Every English colony except Georgia was planted in America in the seventeenth century, a time par excellence of the English trading companies. The economic historian would likely attribute this feverish activity to new commercial forces at work, whereas the political historian would probably ascribe it to the national rivalries existing between Spain, France, Holland and England.

Both explanations would be correct, but also incomplete. As Professor William Warren Sweet clarifies, "Neither of them, nor both together, can explain adequately the establishment of the majority of the English colonies in America. It is true that economic stress was, very probably, responsible for bringing the majority of colonists to America during the whole period of the colonies, but religion was responsible for the founding of more colonies than any other single force."[29]

First Settlers

The Virginia colony, established in Jamestown in 1607, was England's first settlement in America. The Charter of 1606 is a document from King James to the Virginia Company, assigning land rights to colonists for the stated purpose of propagating the Christian religion.

On April 26, 1607, 104 settlers arrived at Cape Henry. Before permitting the settlers to continue looking for a permanent home, their chaplain, Reverend Robert Hunt, required the colonists to wait on the ships for three days of personal examination and repentance. They were to consecrate the land for God's purposes, and Hunt wanted them to be contrite in heart. [30]

Though their ships were small, the settlers carried with them a rough-hewn wooden cross for the purpose of giving glory to God in the endeavor. After the three days, Hunt led the party to the wind-swept shore, where they erected the seven-foot oak cross in the sand. There they held the first formal prayer service in Virginia, in thanksgiving for God's mercy and grace in bringing them safely to this new land.

The Virginia charter made it clear that, while enterprise and prosperity were important goals of the colony, gospel evangelism was the first mission of the settlers. The settlers knew that claiming the land and embracing this hope meant more than occupation. It meant gospel conversions.

The first evidence of these conversions came when a young Native American named Navirans embraced the Gospel and became the first Christian convert of Jamestown. Like Pocahontas, and later Chanco, this former pagan became a beloved member of the community and an instrument of God for peace. Once settled in the fort, the whole company attended regular prayer and services led by Reverend Hunt.

Their leader, Captain John Smith, led the explorations along the rivers of Virginia and the Chesapeake Bay. His writings and maps are considered extremely important in encouraging and supporting colonization in the New World. It was Smith who gave the name New England to the region.

Captain Smith's religious feelings, however conventional, were deeply felt and constantly asserted in his writings. He saw the hand of God at work in his life and believed it had also intervened to save the colonies. He concluded that God, who had thwarted Spanish attempts to settle North America, had reserved that region for the Protestant English. Smith is buried in the Church of St. Sepulchre-without-Newgate, the largest parish church in the city of London.

Reverend Hunt, in turn, was a man of impeccable character and heartfelt faith. Smith described him as "that honest, religious, courageous divine." Hunt was a peacemaker, often bringing harmony to a quarreling group of men. He represented the heart of the mission of the Jamestown colony. Through his personal example, winsome dialogue and spiritual leadership, he worked to make this purpose for colonization a reality at Jamestown.

All authorities, including Governor Edward Maria Wingfield, first president of the Council at Jamestown, and Captain John Smith, who agreed in nothing else, agreed in praise of this worthy man. They wrote: "Our factions were oft qualified, and our wants and greater extremities so comforted that they seemed easy in comparison of what we endured after his memorable death."[31]

Hunt can be remembered today as one of America's true spiritual founding fathers; a heroic figure without whom our first settlement might have perished. He is memorialized at Jamestown Island in a beautiful memorial with the following inscription:

> "He preferred the service of God to every thought of ease at home. He endured every privation, yet none ever heard him repine ... He planted the first Protestant Church in America, and laid down his life in the foundation of Virginia."

Some early laws from the Jamestown settlement indicate the similarities in religious development between Massachusetts Bay and Jamestown. Both colonies were founded, at least on paper, to spread the Christian gospel to the Native Americans. Both colonies had established Churches—Anglican in Virginia; Puritan Congregational in Massachusetts.

Although the notion of 'covenant' was certainly stronger in New England, both colonies understood their colonial experiments in terms of covenant theology. If they were obedient to God's commands, God would bless them. If they were not obedient, God would withhold his blessing. Both colonies needed to interpret natural disasters or Indian invasions as signs of God's punishment.

Religion and the state were closely wed in Jamestown and in New England, mandating church attendance, punishing sins such as adultery, fornication and slander, and treating dissenters harshly. New England's track record on this front is well known: Roger Williams, Anne Hutchinson, the Baptists, and the Quakers were all banished from the colony for their dissenting viewpoints. The government of Jamestown could be just as harsh. Roman Catholic priests, for example, were not permitted to stay in the colony for more than five days.

Though religion didn't permeate the culture of colonial Virginia as it did in New England, neither was Virginia an entirely secular place in the seventeenth century. Alexander Whitaker, for example, a leading minister in Virginia's early history, maintained a regular ministry among the English settlers and never lost his desire to convert the Native Americans. John Rolfe married the legendary Pocahontas in 1614, and prayed daily that he could bring to perfection "so holy a work" that she would share his Christian faith.

Puritans

As for our first Puritan settlers, the Mayflower Compact (1620), specified that, "by the grace of God" the colonies were established "for the glory of God, and advancement of the Christian faith." The Founders later clarified this theocentric social vision with the establishment clause of the First Amendment, which opted for separation of Church and state— not to eliminate the influence of religion in the United States— but to protect its multifarious forms.

In William Bradford's famous narrative *On Plymouth Plantation,* he wrote: "Greater things have been produced by His hand that made all things of nothing, and gives being to all things that are; and as one small candle may light a thousand, so the light here kindled hath shone to many yea in some sort to our whole nation; let the glorious name of Jehovah have all the praise."[32]

One of America's earliest protagonists for freedom of conscience was the rigorist Puritan Roger Williams. Williams came to Massachusetts in 1631 after establishing a reputation as a faithful Puritan preacher in England. He soon found his views diverging from those of the other Puritans, both on the issue of fidelity to the Church of England and on taking land from the Indians.

Williams moved to Rhode Island in 1636, founding the city of Providence in honor of the power that carried him through a brutal winter. Under his direction, Rhode Island became the first place in the North American colonies where freedom of religious worship was defined as a human right for all groups, and where the initial attempt at a separation of the institutions of religion and of the state was made.

Rhode Island was indeed a bold experiment. It was in this colony, under Williams, where, for the first time in modern history, the complete separation of Church and state and the liberty of conscience became fact. At the time of the American Revolution nine of the thirteen colonies had established Churches, six of which were Anglican. Only Rhode Island, Pennsylvania, New York and

Delaware had no religious establishments, and almost complete religious freedom flourished in these states.[33]

Williams's position on "soul liberty" (conscience) and separation of Church and state were decidedly religious. Only God knew the heart, he insisted, and only God could promote a truly spiritual life. That being the case, both ministers and magistrates must protect the relationship between God and his servants on earth. "No person with the said colony," the charter of Rhode Island read, "shall be any wise molested, punished, disquieted or called in question for any differences of opinion in matters of religion."[34]

As for converting the Native Americans by force, Williams believed that such conversions violated Christian principles and were one of the most "monstrous and most inhumane" acts forced upon the native peoples of North and South America. He called forced conversion "Antichristian conversion" that was like compelling "an unwilling spouse— to enter into a forced bed."

John Winthrop, Governor of Massachusetts Bay, died in 1649, as did the eloquent preacher and searcher of souls Thomas Shepard. Two years before Thomas Hooker, a towering figure in early colonialism and founder of Connecticut, had passed away, and, in 1652, the great scholar and apologist of the New England Way (New England Congregationalism), John Cotton, died.

By the middle of the seventeenth century, the only remaining father was the great Puritan Richard Mather. Nearing death and realizing his responsibilities to the next generation, Mather warned against letting worldly concerns come into conflict with the piety and religious conviction that motivated the early settlers. He wished to share the experience of a profoundly religious generation ("better to have begot seven bastards than to have preached without a surplice") that saw dangers ahead.[35]

Attempting to protect against future apathy, Mather wrote: "Experience shows that it is an easy thing in the midst of worldly business to lose the life and power of Religion, that nothing should be left thereof but only the external form— worldliness having eaten out the kernel, and having consumed the very soul and life of godliness".[36]

The point being that New Englanders must —above all people— make their affairs virtuous by being concerned not so much with the "things of this life" as with "the heart wherewith they are done. *For if there is no heart* (emphasis added), even preaching and praying and husbandry and fishing "will be no better than acts of profaneness and ungodliness. With his last voice Richard Mather laid upon the society this injunction, that it exhibit the life and power of religion, no longer in defiance of king and bishop, but in earthly and civil employment."[37]

Chapter Three: The Animating Principle of Puritanism, Augustine

"The one thing that delighted me in Cicero's exhortation was that I should love, and seek, and win, and hold, and embrace, not this or that philosophical school but Wisdom itself." St. Augustine

As part of the Protestant revolution, the animating principle behind Puritanism and its religious roots has an intellectual as well as a spiritual side. Medieval historian Etienne Gilson has called it a "Christian Philosophy, in that it too was a belief, "which, although keeping the two orders formally distinct, nevertheless considers the Christian revelation as an indispensable auxiliary to reason." And while Puritans felt the Schoolmen (i.e., medieval Scholasticism) had betrayed Christianity into the hands of Rome, their scholarship never argued with a large array of inherited beliefs and traditional doctrines.[38]

It is especially interesting, indeed surprising, to read renowned Puritan scholar Perry Miller (*The New England Mind*) on the overarching influence of St. Augustine (354-430 AD) —in respects even more so than Calvin and Luther — on this mode of seventeenth century Christianity that so impacted America's foundational years. Thomas Hooker, for example, held the name of Augustine in such high regard as to continue to call him "Saint," even though this use of the word was generally proscribed as a "Popish corruption."[39]

Miller writes:

> "I venture to call this (Puritan) piety Augustinian, not because it depended directly upon Augustine—though one might demonstrate that he exerted the greatest single influence upon Puritan thought next to that of the Bible itself, and in reality a greater one than did John Calvin— nor because Puritan thought and Augustine's harmonize in every particular...

> "I call it Augustinian simply because Augustine is the arch-exemplar of a religious frame of mind of which Puritanism is one instance out of many in fifteen hundred years of religious history. For a number of reasons many persons in late sixteenth-century England found them- selves looking upon the problems of life very nearly as Augustine viewed them ...

> "In the 1630's some twenty thousand of them, avowedly inspired by their religious views, settled New England and thus served to leave the impress of Augustine upon the sermons, but we can read the inward meaning of all of them in the *Confessions*."[40]

All of which is to say that the separation of Church and state issue, as well as the freedom of conscience issue, have deep theological roots. They reach back many centuries, not only to Augustine but even to pre-Christian times. In his *Confessions*, for example, Augustine attributes his initial movement toward Christianity to Cicero's *Hortensius,* which he considered a philosophical work of the highest rank, pointing him, as he says, toward God himself.

St. Augustine

St. Augustine —brilliant, prolific and profoundly persuasive— is acknowledged by both Protestant and Catholic scholars as one of the founders of Western theology. Historian Philip Schaff writes of him that he is "a philosophical and theological genius of the first order, dominating like a pyramid, antiquity and the succeeding ages. Compared with the great philosophers of past centuries and modern times, he is the equal of them all; among theologians he is undeniably the first, and such has been his influence that none of the Fathers, Scholastics, or Reformers has surpassed it."[41]

Augustine's influence on Christianity is thought by many to be second only to that of St. Paul. John Calvin and the Jansenists were professed followers of Augustine; Martin Luther was an Augustinian monk steeped in the teachings of St. Augustine. It is remarkable that the great critics, Protestant as well as Catholic, are almost unanimous in placing St. Augustine in the foremost ranks of Doctors and proclaiming him the greatest of the Fathers of the Church.

The great Protestant theologian Adolph Harnack (1851-1930), has said of Augustine, "Where in the history of the West, is there to be found a man who, in point of influence can be compared with him. No man since Paul is comparable to him. Even today we live by Augustine, by his thought and his spirit; it is said that we are the sons of the Renaissance and the Reformation, but both one and the other depend on him," noting that, while Luther and Calvin were content to treat Augustine with some indifference, their descendants do him full justice.[42]

In his fourteenth lesson on "The Essence of Christianity," Harnack characterized the Roman Church by three elements, the third of which is Augustinism, the thought and the piety of St. Augustine. "In fact Augustine has exerted over the whole inner life of the Church, religious life and religious thought, an absolutely decisive influence." And again he says, "In the fifth century, at the hour when the Church inherited the Roman Empire, she had within her a man of extraordinarily deep and powerful genius; from him she took her ideas, and to this present hour she has been unable to break away from them."[43]

In his *History of Dogma* Harnack dwells at length on the features of what he calls the "popular Catholicism"[44] to which Augustine belongs, and which so distinguished his views from those of Luther and Calvin. These features include (a) the Church as a hierarchical institution with doctrinal authority; (b) eternal life by merits — that is, salvation by that firm confidence in God which the certainty of pardon produces (and disregard of the Protestant thesis of "salvation by faith") and (c) the forgiveness of sins, — in the Church and by Church.

Harnack notes that Augustine is accused of "outdoing the superstitious ideas" of this popular Catholicism, — such as the infinite value of Christ's satisfaction; salvation considered as enjoyment of God in heaven; the mysterious efficacy of the sacraments (*ex opere operato*, that is, by the power of the sacrament itself); and Mary's virginity even in childbirth, the idea of her purity and her conception, unique in their kind. These are all positions still firmly held by the Catholic Church.

Augustine, writing in the fifth century, is perhaps best known for his major opus, *The City of God,* to which he devoted thirteen years of intellectual labor and study and which has been called a masterpiece. Except for his *Confessions,* it is the best known and most widely read of his works, and was the only philosophy of history throughout Europe during the Middle Ages.

The City of God is highly respected among numerous Protestant writers. Even the skeptical Gibbon, who had no sympathy for the religion and theology of Augustine, concedes at least "the merit of a magnificent design, vigorously, and not unskillfully, executed."[45]

The City of God's effect can be discerned in the writings of the Founders and impacts Catholic political thought even today. It was endorsed, for example, by the scholarly Pope Leo XIII in his encyclical letter *On the Christian Constitution of States (Immortale Dei).* Here Pope Leo says that Augustine "set forth so clearly the efficacy of Christian wisdom and the way in which it is bound up with the well-being of states, that he seems not only to have pleaded the cause of Christianity in his own time, but to have triumphantly refuted the false charges (against Christianity) forever."[46]

In this masterwork Augustine argues that, at a minimum, the state should not hinder the free practice of the Christian faith. Not unlike many of the Founders, Augustine felt the state should, in fact, help advance religion. At the same time he realized the more modest goal of a secular but virtuous state would be more likely, which was precisely what the Founders had in mind in vigorously supporting free religious exercise.

Augustine, in the *Confessions,* describes the seminal moment in his young and turbulent life that is relevant to his later political insights, anticipating especially the need for virtuous conduct. He was then only eighteen years old. Dismayed and frustrated by the skeptical rhetoricians of his time and caught up in a lustful life-style—he describes himself as "wretched" — he discovers Cicero's dialogue *Hortensius*.

And he writes, "Quite definitely it changed the direction of my mind, altered my prayers to You, O Lord, and gave me a new purpose and ambition. Suddenly all the vanity I had hoped in I saw as worthless, and with an incredible intensity of desire I longed after immortal wisdom."[47]

What could it possibly be in the pre-Christian, pagan Cicero (106-43 B.C.) that transformed the life of Augustine, impacted such post-Renaissance thinkers as Locke, Hume and Montesquieu, and extended even to the generation of our founding fathers?

In his early philosophical dialogues *Contra Academico, De Beata Vita,* and *De Ordine,* written while he was preparing for baptism, Augustine acknowledges his respect for Cicero on virtually every page. He was convinced that behind the mask of the skeptic in Cicero was the mind and heart of a seeker after truth.[48]

Cicero

Cicero, it turns out, is Augustine's link to authentic philosophy and genuine love of wisdom. "It was to philosophy that that book set me so ardently," he writes in the *Confessions*. And it wasn't just any philosophy. It wasn't the sophism, relativism and agnosticism of the Carthage school that he found. As he writes: "The one thing that delighted me in Cicero's exhortation was that I should love, and seek, and win, and hold, and embrace, not this or that philosophical school but Wisdom itself, whatever it might be. The book

(*Hortensius*) excited and inflamed me; in my ardour the only thing I found lacking was that the name of Christ was not there."[49]

It is in Augustine's discovery of Cicero, the prominent Roman statesman and moral and political philosopher, that he finds for the first time an iteration of the universal basis of justice and rights and the timeless language of natural law. Cicero, in turn, was greatly influenced by the metaphysics of Aristotle; centuries later Dante would look back on Cicero as Rome's "best Aristotelian."

As for our Founders, Jefferson explicitly names Cicero as one of a handful of major figures who contributed to the tradition of "the public right" that informed his draft of the Declaration of Independence and shaped American understanding of "the common sense" basis for the right of revolution."[50]

Scholar James Reid writes of Cicero that he "stands out as a patriotic Roman of substantial honesty, who gave his life to check the inevitable fall of the commonwealth to which he was devoted. The evils which were undermining the Republic bear so many striking resemblances to those which threaten the civic and national life of America today that the interest of the period is by no means merely historical."[51]

As for Augustine, we might say he is intellectually armed by Cicero, in effect baptizing him and providing his own later theological writings a philosophical underpinning of unparalleled strength and historical influence. As is well known, Augustine is the pre-eminent Father of the Church, a true luminary of early Christian thought. What is lesser appreciated is his inspiration among leading thinkers through the Renaissance, post-Renaissance, the Protestant Reformation, and into the foundational times of our country.

Already in the fifth century we see the influence of Augustine on the relationship of Church and state. Less than 100 years after Augustine, Pope Gelasius I, following in his tradition, wrote to the emperor Anastasius in Constantinople in AD 494:

> "There are two powers—by which this world is chiefly ruled, namely the sacred authority of the priests, and the royal power. Of these, that of the priests is more weighty, since they have to render an account for even the kings of men in the divine judgment. You are also aware, dear son, that while you are permitted honorably to rule over human kind, yet in things divine you bow your head humbly before the leaders of the clergy and await from their hands the means of salvation."[52]

Augustine, Grace and Freedom

It is especially important to study Augustine in the context of Protestantism —the dominant religious force in the founding of this country— and the relationship of grace and freedom. A richer understanding of this relationship, both on what we might call the personal or *vertical* plane (each man's relationship to God) as well as the cultural, or *horizontal* plane (society's openness to God) is indispensable to the authentic vision and development of democracies going forward. Especially, we might add, given the evidence of their profound religious roots.

The first thing to say about this grace-freedom relationship— acknowledged by both Luther and Catholicism and which, in fact, is a divine-human relationship since grace is from God and freedom is man's response—is that God's actions precede man's. Its formal Catholic expression is: "Grace is first and foremost the gift of the

Spirit who justifies and sanctifies us,"[53] and "preparation of man for the reception of grace is already a work of grace."[54]

But the Church goes on to clarify that "God's free initiative *demands man's free response*, for God has created man in his image by conferring on him, along with freedom, the power to know him and love him. The soul only enters *freely* into the communion of love. God immediately touches and directly moves the heart of man."[55]

Nurturing this relationship on the personal level is obviously a fundamental challenge for man and requires an appropriate use of his freedom. Man, after all, is given great tasks that he must be empowered to pursue. He must not only "be fruitful and multiply, fill the earth and subdue it," (Gen.1:27-28), which we might call a horizontal task, but along the vertical line he is also called "to be perfect, therefore, as your heavenly father is perfect."[56]

These are truly grand tasks and they are not meant to be solitary or non-relational. They are not a matter of man working alone and God looking on, as the deists would have it. Nor are they Pelagian, requiring a strong dose of free will but without the need for divine aid in performing good works.

Rather, grace and freedom are the soul of a marvelous joint-venture, indeed an *adventure* of man with God, of Father with son, with true significance for this world and with a destiny beyond it. They represent a journey the Founders embraced with an intensity of faith and a magnanimity of soul that too often seems lost on the children— not to mention the leadership— of this generation.

Lest we forget the first great commandment—loving God with one's whole mind, heart, soul and strength — it is the primary task of freedom to be properly disposed to the divine, such that one's actions

35

are abetted by God's grace. To deny this freedom to love is to deny a primordial teaching of Christianity. It would be, to use a Thomistic metaphor, like stubbornly walking about with one's eyes closed and believing the world is dark, when in fact the sun is shining. We are free to open our eyes and be guided by the light— or not.

A great challenge to seeing the world and man's vocation in this light is to believe, as did Luther, that, due to original sin, man is essentially corrupt. He simply cannot see—*because he is without freedom.* Nature has been debased at its very core by this primeval turning from God and, even under grace, it remains debased and impotent. As we shall see, St. Augustine provides an indispensable clarification to this tragic misunderstanding.

Luther read and studied a wide range of Augustine's writings, memorized passages from them, and cited Augustine more than any other non-scriptural source. He initially made his own the basic tenets of Augustine's theology, as evidenced by his work as a professor at the University of Wittenberg. Even after the public eruption of the Protestant Reformation in 1517, Luther continued to selectively (and sometimes out of context) quote the writings of Augustine, and continued to praise him even after disagreeing in matters regarding authority and the magisterium of the Church.

In their long introduction to Luther's *Bondage of the Will*, which he considered his most important work, authors James I. Packer and O.R. Johnston quote Luther consistently making the point that there is no free will, at least twice insisting that we cannot do any-thing to get grace.[57]

At one point, Luther compares a human being to a horse: either God or the devil will ride the person, and, unfortunately, the person has nothing to say as to which one rides him. So he goes to heaven or hell accordingly (predestination), and has no control over which place he goes. It is indeed a dismal picture; for Luther goes on to say God saves "so few and damns so many." [58]

Yet—somehow— Luther says we must show "some measure of deference" to His Wisdom. We must *think* He is just when He seems unjust—the irrationality of which greatly disturbed Luther himself. He acknowledges it caused him to go down to "the deepest pit of despair," even wishing he had not been made a man.[59]

Unfortunately, man is then, as the esteemed Thomist philosopher Jacques Maritain puts it, a "walking corruption; but this irremediably corrupt nature cries to God, and the initiative, do what one will, is thus *man's by that cry*."[60] It is a schema in which grace is not a "new life" of the soul, as the Church teaches, but only a covering cloak. Freedom has become a lost power and is now irrelevant. Due to Adam's fall, man's free will has been killed by original sin.

Man thus finds himself in a great paradox: he is solely in God's power— and yet he must act. So he, not God, must take the initiative. Man is thus called to exercise a freedom— that he appears not to have! And of course he *does* act, as daily life and common sense show, and as Luther recognized. But these actions, rather than reflecting a "religion of the Spirit" and response to grace, as Louis Bouyer points out, become an affirmation that lies at the root of liberal Protestantism. Namely a denial of grace, a self-assertion of the individual and a subjectivizing of religion.

"Thus," Bouyer continues, "it has to be admitted that the affirmation that lies at the root of Protestantism, of this 'liberalism' in its true and final expression, *must be the self-assertion of the individual*. This involves an individualism that rejects not only the affirmations of the Christian community of tradition but any divine revelation not made directly to the individual consciousness."[61]

"Wherever liberal Protestantism has gained the upper hand, Protestantism is but an aggregate of different religious forms of free thought."[62] Little wonder, then, that modern Protestantism has moved far from Luther's untenable positions.

Bouyer makes a critical clarification, however, that is highly relevant to the thesis of this book, namely the evangelical, Christian roots of democracy. He is careful to point out that this "codified" and liberal presentation of Protestantism is not in fact its "living religion." It isn't Protestantism "in the souls where it is alive," as he puts it, and so to take the 'liberal' version for living Protestantism "is to be entirely mistaken."[63]

As his book explores, "we will soon find that Protestantism, for its members, means not private judgment but *biblical Christianity,* incomplete or illogical it may be, but yet it is authentically religious."[64] And as we see in its most distinguished figures over time, it is this Christianity —incomplete perhaps but deeply embraced — that has been such a living force in the formation of our country. This will be of great import in the challenge of contemporary society going forward, namely to rediscover the fullness of its marvelously rich and dynamic Christian spirit.

Bouyer notes that, in one sense, as Catholic teaching would have it, Luther's dogmatic position is true—grace does not originate with man. His great failure is not to recognize Augustine's clarification regarding freedom, namely the freedom man *must* have—and that the state must not violate— in order to correspond to the grace bestowed on him.

And it is not, then, so much the 'doctrinal' Protestantism' of Luther and Calvin but the living Christianity of Augustine—we might call it an authentically religious Christianity *by inspiration* or a Christianity of the Spirit—that so forcefully impacted the founding of this country, and that is so in need of rediscovery in modern times.

Such is the meaning, (briefly, to be sure) of the doctrines of pre-destination and reprobation as understood by the various schools of Protestantism: the theology of *grace without freedom.* This is the doctrine of Luther, of Calvin, and of Jansenius. Augustine, from a certain non-theological perspective, may seem to agree with this very constrained perspective of man's relationship to God.

In fact, however, he does not agree, which no doubt explains some of his appeal to the Protestant founding fathers, who so highly valued both freedom and rationality. Augustine defends first principles and free will by showing that it is absurd to deny them and any challenge to them. For him, free will is implied in every moral judgment, whether that judgment be God's or our own.

Rewards and punishments, either human or divine, would be unjust if those rewarded or punished were not responsible for their actions, that is, free to have done or not to have done them.

Our moral, political and religious lives would be absurd—completely devoid of justice and responsibility—if there were no free will. Put more radically, human judgment *requires* freedom of choice. Even to challenge the justice of God's punishment implies freedom of choice.

If I challenge, then I am free. If I am offended by the injustice of God, then I am free.

According to St. Thomas Aquinas, the most authentic interpreter of the thought of St. Augustine and an echo of the whole Catholic tradition, concupiscence is only the *material* element of original sin. Its persistence in us in no way prevents original sin from being effaced by baptism, and sanctifying grace from residing intrinsically in our soul.[65]

The *formal* element of original sin, per Aquinas, is the ruptured relationship between God and man —the loss of justification—which can only be healed by the grace of God. "Grace is *favor,* the *free and undeserved* help that God gives us to respond to his call to become children of God, adoptive sons, partakers of the divine nature and of eternal life."[66]

It is the opinion of St. Augustine that "the justification of the wicked is a greater work than the creation of heaven and earth," because "heaven and earth will pass away but the salvation and justification of the elect ... will not pass away."[67] Augustine also held that the "justification of sinners surpasses the creation of the angels in justice, in that it bears witness to a greater mercy."[68]

Here it might be noted that, generally speaking on any question of sacred theology that presents a Thomistic synthesis, Aquinas is in wholehearted faithfulness to Augustine. And, as Maritain notes, "Everyone knows that the main doctrine in which their agreement is manifest is the doctrine of grace."[69]

Maritain writes, "When St. Thomas teaches the motion of the human free will by grace and divine causality in such a way that the free mode of our voluntary acts is itself caused by God, and that all their goodness comes, at once from God as first cause and from us as second cause, and that we are the first cause only of evil—it is the very voice of St. Augustine and of St. Paul to whom we are listening."[70]

And he continues: "St. Augustine taught as clearly as possible the ontological value of the distinction between nature and grace ... and that even in the angels grace is distinct from nature."[71] Which is to say— to clarify Luther's position— man cannot replace God. He cannot, on his own initiative, *do anything divine*. It is grace that "divinizes" man.

In return for his grace, God's expectation is man's free response, "for God has created man in his image by conferring on him, along with freedom, the power to know him and love him. The soul only enters *freely* into the communion of love. God immediately touches and directly moves the heart of man. He has placed in man a longing for truth and goodness that only he can satisfy. The promises of 'eternal life' respond, beyond all hope, to this desire."[72]

In the words of Augustine, "If at the end of your very good works— you rested on the seventh day, it was to foretell by the voice of your book that at the end of our works, which are indeed 'very good' since you have given them to us, we shall rest in you on the sabbath of eternal life."[73]

Despite its perhaps ecumenical incorrectness, in reflecting on Luther's *sola fide*—or 'faith saving without good works,' —we have St. Thomas noting that "he who (duly enlightened) refuses his adherence to the magisterium of the Church, even on a single point, loses theological faith by that act."[74] Wherein, of course, lies the great Reformation divide and the seeds of separation of faith and culture so endemic to modern times.

Calvinism

For the Reformers, original sin is not just a sin, it is *the* sin. It is a *permanent* sin that lives in us and causes a continual stream of new sins to spring from our nature, which is radically corrupt and evil.

Calvin puts it this way: "Let it stand, therefore, as an indubitable truth which no engines can shake, that the mind of man is so entirely alienated from the righteousness of God that he cannot conceive, desire or design anything but what is weak, distorted, foul, impure or iniquitous, that his heart is so thoroughly environed by sin that it can breathe out nothing but corruption and rottenness; that if some men occasionally make a show of goodness their mind is ever interwoven with hypocrisy and deceit, their soul inwardly bound with the fetter of wickedness."[75]

Calvin's way out of this horrible theory is, of course, predestination. Divine predestination from all eternity separates the elect, who are to be snatched out of the mass of perdition, from the reprobates who are destined to hell. For Calvin, man is faced with the same challenge: he is bound down —almost annihilated — under despotic forces. But— the predestined one is sure of salvation. He can thus act as the elect of God on earth and, due to his exalted state, his material prosperity will seem to him a right. He and God stand together, as it were, at the wheel of his ship of destiny.

Today there is an almost unanimous rejection by Protestants of what they themselves call "the boldest defiance ever given to reason and conscience."[76] The Calvinist dogma is today, especially in England, altogether abandoned and often replaced by pure Pelagianism and a pointing toward the Catholic interpretation of St. Augustine.

As Maritain importantly notes, under Calvinism and the ship of destiny, "so far as the direction is in (man's) hands it is *not in the hands of God."* (emphasis added) This inevitably leads to an anthropocentric (and mistaken) humanism, whereby man believes in God and in grace but feels *he* must take the primary initiative regarding salvation and actions that merit eternal life.[77]

God is thus, in reality, out of the picture. And so this self-deified man, solely on his own initiative, must undertake to look after matters dealing with the earthly life and happiness. One can readily find, in this attitude, the seeds of the radical individualism and, eventually, the diminution of faith and flattening of religious experience that are so pronounced in contemporary American culture.

Anthropocentric or man-centered humanism, says Maritain, leads to an ambivalence and confusion regarding the relationship of grace and freedom. Ultimately, it presents a pure Protestant theology of grace without freedom, conjoined to a humanistic metaphysics or theology of freedom without grace—meaning freedom without God. Both of which are, in their own way, symptomatic and indeed causative of the agnostic humanism of modern times.

Thus man alone is the maker of his destiny. With science and technology at his command, with economics as his incentive and the dynamic of inevitable progress as his *weltanschauung,* he is able to meet all contingencies. He is like a god, able to control the conduct of his own life and the operation of the great universe as well.[78] All of which leads, in practice, to a humanistic agnosticism that doesn't really need God—and leads inexorably to an individual and communal loss of faith and the "naked public square" so aptly described by Fr. Richard J. Neuhaus.

As for Calvin, no one is as influential in his writing as St. Augustine. His first work, *Commentary on Seneca's De Clementia* (1532), includes Augustine among the most esteemed philosophers, poets and historians, such as Cicero, Horace, Ovid and Plutarch. In his fifteen references to the Fathers, thirteen are to Augustine. Calvin's interest in and use of Augustine were enduring and constant in all his writings, quoting him 50 percent more than of all his other patristic references.

The linkage between Calvin and Augustine is important here in demonstrating the rich theological and historical trajectory of American democracy. As many as two-thirds of the 3 million people living at the time of the American Revolution had their theological roots in Calvinism.[79] The great German historian Leopold von Ranke viewed Calvin as "the virtual founder of America;" the leading American historian of the nineteenth century, George Bancroft, called him "the Father of America."

From 1551 to 1556, Calvin completed a number of New Testament commentaries in which the most frequently quoted Church Father is Augustine. Little wonder Calvin called Augustine "the greatest theologian" who had comprehensively grasped all the doctrines of the Scriptures and who is the best-qualified representative of the Church of the early centuries. By his own proclamation Calvin said of Augustine, *"Augustinus totus noster est"*—Augustine is absolutely on our side!" [80]

It is thus fair to say that the unusual influence of Augustine on both Luther and Calvin carried well into the founding years of the American republic. At the same time it should be noted that the

Catholic Church, principally through the Council of Trent (1545-1563), maintained pure Augustinianism in the bosom of the Church. Against Pelagianism it did this by reaffirming original sin and the absolute necessity of grace. And against Protestant predestination it did it by reaffirming the freedom of man, with his double power of resisting grace and of doing good or evil, even before embracing the Faith. [81]

Jansen

As for Jansenism, which has been called "Catholic Puritanism," Jansenius's (1585-1638) three- volume major opus *Augustinus* took him twenty years to write. Its research involved reading the whole of Augustine ten times, and his treatise against the Pelagians thirty times. The success of the *Augustinus* —published posthumously — was great, and it spread rapidly throughout Belgium, Holland and France. (Jansen never broke with Catholicism; he lived and died in the bosom of the Church. At the time of his promotion to the doctorate in 1619, he had defended categorically the infallibility of the Pope.)[82]

Jansenism, however, was a different story. It denied freedom of the will, accepted supernatural determinism (predestination), and emphasized puritanical moral attitudes, maintaining that human nature is incapable of good. In 1641, a decree of the Holy Office condemned Jansen's work and prohibited its reading. The following year, Pope Urban renewed the condemnation.

A major contribution of Augustine to Puritanism was reinforcing the revelation of the fundamental norms of the natural law to the chosen People. Augustine notes that the Decalogue is the summary and epitome of all laws. "Although the Lord has spoken many things, He gave to Moses (Ex. 31:18; 32:15) only two stone tablets, called 'tables of testimony' to be placed in the Ark. For if carefully explained and well understood, whatever else is commanded by God will be found to depend on the Ten Commandments which were engraved on those two tables, just as these Ten Commandments, in turn, are reducible to two, the love of God and of our neighbor, on which depends the whole law and the prophets."[83]

As for Puritanism's debt to Scholasticism, the scholastics supplied content for every department of Puritan thought.

Miller writes:

> "Though Puritan literature abounds with condemnation of Scholasticism, almost no limit can be set to its actual influence. At every turn we encounter ideas and themes which descend, by whatever stages, from medieval philosophy, while the forms of the thinking, the terminology, the method of logic—though this was believed to have been drastically revolutionized in the sixteenth century—were still duplications of medieval habits, modified but not transformed. Indeed, in seventeenth-century Puritanism, the scholastic influence was actually stronger than it had been in sixteenth-century Protestantism, and for the same reasons that dictated the exaltation of 'method.'

> Although John Preston recommended that students come to scholastic philosophy after they had studied a Protestant compendium, yet he was himself a great reader of Scotus, Occam and particularly of Aquinas, 'whose *Summa* he would sometimes read as the Barber cut his

hair, and when it fell upon the place he read, he would not lay down his book, but blow it off.'"[84]

John Cotton wrote in 1652—in a passage indispensable to understanding New England's intellectual history— "The Schoolmen (though they be none of the soundest Divines) yet of late years, have crept (for a time) into more credit amongst Schools, then the most judicious and orthodox of our best writers (Luther, Calvin, Martyr, Bucer, and the rest) and their books were much more vendible (*salable*), and at a far greater price."[85]

Miller, while acknowledging the debt to Calvin of Harvard theologians of the seventeenth century, notes that:

> "The scholars had chiefly to take into account classical literature, brought into prominence by the humanists, and the literature of scholastic science and philosophy. When they were appropriating heathen material for Christian purposes they were still faithful to the precepts of Augustine, who had said that we should 'claim it for our own use from those who have unlawful possession of it,' but they were all the more eager for the capture because to them it seemed that the revival of 'the Gentile learning' and the reformation of religion had gone hand in hand. As always, providence was at work in the course of human history, but in this case it had managed affairs with even more than its usual dexterity."[86]

One might best sum up Miller's view of the Puritan era in his own words: "I am prepared to hazard the thesis that whatever may be the case in other centuries, in the sixteenth and seventeenth certain men of decisive importance took religion seriously; that they often followed spiritual dictates in comparative disregard of ulterior considerations ..."[87]

As for Miller's quality of scholarship, the body of published sources relevant to New England, both here and in Europe, for the period 1620 to 1730, amounted to about 1,500 titles. Of these, in *The New England Mind,* volumes one and two, Miller cites 223 titles—15 percent of the total— and had read far more.[88]

H. Richard Niebuhr called *The New England Mind* "a magnificent book, the most illuminating and convincing interpretation of Puritanism that I know..." James Hoopes said this classic work "towers over the great mass of subsequent scholarship, and remains after forty years our best single best work on American Puritanism." Mark Noll has called Miller "one of the twentieth century's greatest historians."[89]

Chapter Four: Pre-British History

"Without morals a republic cannot subsist any length of time; they therefore who are decrying the Christian religion ... are undermining the solid foundation of morals, the best security for the duration of free governments." Charles Carroll

A s a relevant aside, we as a nation are also inclined to ignore our pre-British history. The fact is that the people of this land were called Christians before they were called Americans. There were already Christian influences in Florida in the 1520s and in California in the 1540s.

The first Catholic settlement was in St. Augustine, Florida in 1565. Well before the British settlement in Jamestown (1607), thousands of Native Americans had become at least nominal believers under Catholic missionaries in the New Mexico territories.

St. Augustine, Florida

The vicinity of St. Augustine, Florida was first explored in 1513 by Spanish explorer Ponce de Leon, just twenty years after Columbus's great discovery. Prior to the founding of St. Augustine in 1565, several earlier attempts at European colonization of what is now Florida were made by both Spain and France, but all failed. It was named by Don Pedro Menendez de Aviles, Florida's governor, who arrived off the coast of Florida on August 28, 1565, the Feast of St. Augustine.[90]

Thus, St. Augustine was founded more than four decades before the English colony at Jamestown, Virginia, and fifty-five years before the Pilgrims landed on Plymouth Rock, making it the oldest permanent European settlement in North America.

> *Martín de Argüelles is on record as the first European born in the continental United States, in San Augustin in 1566. The first black child born here, in the year 1606, was Augustin—thirteen years before enslaved Africans were first brought to Jamestown in 1619.*

St. Augustine was intended as a base for further colonial ventures across what is now the southeastern United States. Such efforts were hampered, however, by apathy and hostility on the part of the Native Americans toward becoming Spanish subjects.

In 1668, St. Augustine was attacked and plundered by Robert Searle, an English privateer. Four years later, in the aftermath of his raid, the Spanish began the construction of a more secure fortification— the Castillo de San Marcos— which still stands today as the nation's oldest fort.

The Spanish had fewer slaves in Florida than the English Americans in the colonies, since it was basically a military outpost rather than a plantation economy. And as British settlements moved farther south, the Spanish began giving sanctuary to slaves who could escape from British plantations and make their way to Florida, thus becoming the focal point of the first Underground Railroad.

Blacks were given sanctuary, arms and supplies if they joined the Catholic Church and swore allegiance to the king of Spain. As the British established settlements closer to Spanish territory, with Charleston in 1670 and Savannah in 1733, Spanish governor Manual de Montiano in 1738 established the first legally recognized free community of ex-slaves as the northern defense of St. Augustine, known as Gracia Real de Santa Teresa de Mose, or Fort Mose.

In 1740, St. Augustine was unsuccessfully attacked by British forces from their colonies in the Carolinas and Georgia. The largest of these was organized by Governor James Oglethorpe of Georgia, who managed to break the Spanish-Seminole alliance with the help of a Seminole tribal chief.

In the subsequent campaign, Oglethorpe, supported by several thousand colonial militia and British regulars along with Seminole warriors, invaded Spanish Florida and conducted the Siege of St. Augustine during the War of Jenkin's Ear. During this siege, the black community of St. Augustine proved its worth by stopping the city's take-over by the British.

The leader of Fort Mose during the battle was the legendary Capt. Francisco Menendez, a Creole born in Africa who had twice escaped from slavery and played an important role in defending St. Augustine from British raids. The Fort Mose site is now recognized as a National Historic Landmark.

Junipero Serra, California

The famous Blessed Junipero Serra founded the mission of San Francisco in 1776, the year of the signing of the Declaration of Independence. (A bronze statue of Fr. Serra, representing the state of California, can be found in the National Hall of Statuary in Washington).[91]

Father Serra had been appointed superior of a band of fifteen Franciscans in 1767 for the Indian Missions of Lower California. Early in 1769, he accompanied Portolá's land expedition to Upper California and, on the way, established the Mission San Fernando de Velicatá, Lower California.

Serra arrived at San Diego on the first of July, and on July 16 founded the first of the twenty-one California missions that enabled the conversions of the coastal natives as far north as Sonoma. Missions established by Father Serra or during his administration were San Carlos on June 3, 1770; San Antonio on July 14, 1771; San Gabriel on September 8, 1771; San Luis Obispo on September 1, 1772; San Francisco de Asis on October 8, 1776; San Juan Capistrano on November 1, 1776; Santa Clara on January 12, 1777 and San Buenaventura on March 31, 1782.

Father Serra was also present at the founding of the *presidio* of Santa Barbara on April 21, 1782 and was prevented from locating the mission there only because of the animosity of Governor Filipe de Neve. During the final three years of his life Father Serra once more visited the missions from San Diego to San Francisco, extending 600 miles. In the process he confirmed more than 5,000 Indians who, since his arrival in 1770, had converted to Christianity.

Along with extraordinary fortitude, Father Serra's most conspicuous virtues were an insatiable zeal, a great love of mortification (he suffered intensely from his crippled leg and from his chest, yet would use no remedies), a generous self-denial and an absolute confidence in God.

Father Serra's executive abilities have been especially noted by non-Catholic writers. Mrs. Leland Stanford, for example, wife of the founder of the university and deeply religious, had a granite monument erected to him at Monterey. A bronze statue of heroic size in Golden Gate Park, San Francisco, represents him as the apostolic preacher.

In 1884 the Legislature of California passed a concurrent resolution making August 29 of that year— the centennial of Father Serra's burial— a legal holiday. Junipero Serra was beatified by Pope John Paul II on September 25, 1988.

First Institutions

All of this is simply to remind ourselves—somewhat ironically perhaps, given the HHS mandate in violation of Catholic teaching and freedom of conscience—that the first well-established institutions in the New World came from the work of Catholics.

The first printed hymnbook in America, sometimes thought to be the Puritan's *Bay Psalm Book* of 1640, was in fact the *Ordinary of the Mass* in Mexico City in 1556. It featured music next to the words, which British-American hymnals didn't incorporate until the eighteenth century.

Protestant influence on the United States cannot be minimized. As historian Paul Johnson succinctly put it, America was "born Protestant," and any objective reading of American history demonstrates that Calvinism (versus, say, Lutheranism or any other theological system) had the most significant and widespread impact on the thinking of early Americans.[92]

At the same time names such as St. Augustine and San Antonio, Los Angeles, Vincennes, Marquette, Louisville and so many others, serve to remind us that there were earlier arrivals. And that their influence and that of their descendants —now the largest Christian denomination in the United States—is a vibrant part of American history.[93]

The colony of Maryland was founded by a charter granted in 1632 to George Calvert, secretary of state to Charles I and his son Cecil, both recent converts to Catholicism. Its most famous early father was Charles Carroll of Carrollton, the longest-lived (and last surviving) signatory of the Declaration of Independence and the only Catholic.

In 1634, a mix of Catholic and Protestant settlers arrived at St. Clement's Island in Southern Maryland at the invitation of the Catholic Lord Baltimore. While Catholics and Protestants were killing each other in Europe, Lord Baltimore imagined Maryland as a society where people of different faiths could live together peacefully.

Baltimore's vision was soon codified in Maryland's 1649 *Act Concerning Religion* (also called the "Toleration Act"), which was the first law in our nation's history to protect an individual's right to freedom of conscience.

As for Carroll, he was a great champion of religious liberty and the most vocal Catholic of his time to demand this basic freedom. At the time of the signing of the Declaration, Carroll pledged his fortune to the cause.[94] Though elected to the Continental Congress from Maryland, the only nominally Catholic colony and with a history of religious tolerance, Carroll was denied an official seat at the assembly because of his religion.

Despite his firm Catholic convictions, Carroll wrote of Christianity in general: "Without morals a republic cannot subsist any length of time; they therefore who are decrying the Christian religion, whose morality is so sublime and pure ... are undermining the solid foundation of morals, the best security for the duration of free governments."[95]

How unfortunate if such nobility of character, clarity of vision and strength of faith would be lost to the sands of time. In reflecting on the Catholic and Christian history of this country, one feels compelled to ask: Would we not be well-served to better remember our past and such remarkable men as Charles Carroll and our other forefathers? Not just to recollect but to take inspiration from them as to how best to advance this special nation—the 'city on the hill' (Mt 5:14) foreseen by John Winthrop—and its precious freedoms.

Chapter Five: The Great Awakening

It is from the "sense of spiritual beauty" that there arises "all true experimental knowledge of religion and indeed a whole new world of knowledge." Jonathan Edwards

A spiritual event in the first half of the eighteenth century, the Great Awakening, proved of large significance to this country from both a political and a religious perspective.[96] It was to leave a major mark on the development of democracy and religion in American history.

Responding in part to the decline of Puritanism and the weakening power of the old Calvinist doctrines, the Great Awakening might be described as a Christian revitalization movement. It swept both Protestant Europe and British America and had a particular impact on the pre-Revolutionary American colonies in the 1730s and 1740s.

It could be argued that the specifically American form of Christianity—undogmatic, moralistic and interior rather than creedal; tolerant but strong and all-pervasive of society—was born in the eighteenth century and that the Great Awakening was its midwife.[97]

The Awakening drew back, as it were, from the ritual and ceremony of Reformation Protestantism. Instead, by encouraging introspection and a high standard of personal morality, it fostered a deep sense of spiritual conviction, redemption and religious inspiration. It placed emphases on the interiorization of religion, on divine outpourings of the Holy Spirit, and conversions among new believers that led to a more intense love for God.[98]

And one of its greatest protagonists was the dynamic minister of the Congregationalist Church in Northampton, Massachusetts, Jonathan Edwards.

Jonathan Edwards

Jonathan Edwards (1703-1758), was the leading American theologian of the colonial era and a 'precursor of the Revolution.'[99] A man of "outstanding intellect and sensibility," he has been called "the first major thinker in American history."[100] Graduating first in his class at Yale, Edwards was to take over his grandfather's church in Northampton, where he attracted a large following with powerfully-delivered sermons.

Edwards put an entirely new gloss on the harsh old Calvinist doctrine of Redemption. He could deliver a hellfire sermon, to be sure. But he preferred to preach of an interior, subjective response to God. To a God who didn't just choose some and not others, but radiated His own goodness and beauty into souls so they could become more like Him. It is a grace; Edwards called it a "kind of participation in God"—Aquinas would call it a "knowledge by connaturality"—in which "God puts his own beauty, i.e., his beautiful likeness, upon their souls."

> As an aside, for Aquinas grace is not considered a "substance" of the soul— it is not part of the soul's nature. The soul obtains grace through a *participation* in the Divine goodness. Thus, what is substantial in God becomes accidental in the soul by participation. Grace can be considered as simply a participation, though imperfect, in this divine goodness.[101]

> This participation, of course, is no small thing. Aquinas reminds us that: *"the being of an accident is to inhere."* Thus, accidents are said to have being inasmuch as "by them something is." Therefore accidents *belong* to beings, but are not called "beings." Properly speaking, then, no accident comes into being or is corrupted. However, the subject of an accident can begin or cease to be in act while having this accident. "And thus grace is said to be created inasmuch as men are created [anew] with reference to it, i.e., are given a new being out of nothing, i.e. not from merits, according to Eph. 2, 10, *(but) created in Jesus Christ in good works."*[102]

In a *Treatise Concerning the Religious Affections* (1746) Edwards listed in detail the twelve signs by which true religious love could be distinguished. The most important of these was the ability to detect "divine things" by "the beauty of their moral excellency." Echoing Aquinas's notions of connaturality and "grace perfecting nature," Edwards taught that it was from the "sense of spiritual beauty" that there arises "all true experimental knowledge of religion and indeed a whole new world of knowledge."[103]

Most importantly, from the perspective of conscience, in his celebrated *The Freedom of the Will* (1754) Edwards insisted that conscience must be protected because human beings are free. All must be prayed for—nothing is determined in advance. All can choose: We act according to our perceptions and convictions of the good, and God will hold us accountable for our choices.

According to American historian Norman Fiering, Thomas Aquinas was "very well known in early seventeenth-century philosophy and was cited occasionally in student notebooks that have survived from Harvard in this period."[104] One can find in Edwards' thought, and more broadly in seventeenth and eighteenth-century Reformed theology, the influence of Aquinas. Edwards shared some important convictions about salvation with St. Thomas, including assertions about grace and divine initiative as well as the (rather non-Protestant and anti-Lutheran) view that—through grace — real, *ontological* changes take place in the souls of believers.

Solomon Stoddard, Edwards's grandfather, was an influential religious leader in colonial New England. His ideas covered a wide variety of topics, often contrasting with mainstream Puritan thought and foreshadowing modern theological thought. Stoddard owned several of Thomas's works and one of a later Thomist, Francis Suarez.[105] Opponents sometimes referred to him as "Pope" Stoddard, rhetorically placing him in the locally detested camp of the Roman Catholic Church.

Stoddard insisted that the sacrament of the Lord's Supper should be available to all who lived outwardly pious lives and had a good reputation in the community, even if they weren't full members of the Church. This was his attempt to save his Church from a "dying religion," and was the cause of great theological controversy in eighteenth-century New England. Some historians have praised Stoddard for his democratic tendencies (in opening up the Lord's

Supper), while others have condemned him for being anti-democratic by proposing tighter outside controls for local Churches.[106]

As for Edwards, he saw in the regenerate, as he called them, the Holy Spirit operating according to its divine nature, communicating its own holiness to these souls and sanctifying them. The "Gift" of the Spirit, therefore, is not only "from the Spirit, but it also partakes of the nature of that Spirit. The third person of the Trinity is directly and immediately present in the regenerate, just as it is in the immanent Trinity."

Therefore, grace in the soul, Edwards writes, "is the Holy Ghost acting in the soul, and communicating his own holy nature," or "the very Holy Ghost dwelling in the souls acting there as a vital principle."[107]

The significance of all this is that, to the extent that the Reformation was soteriological (that is, involving salvation), the preeminent theologian of the colonial era—Jonathan Edwards—finds the basis or "root" of justification, not in the Reformation position of the righteousness of Christ outside of us or of grace *wholly extrinsic to us*, but rather in the Catholic view of grace as the work of God *in us*.[108]

A work, we might add, that we are free to respond to or not. Hence, the grave importance of a well-developed and free conscience; such consequential decisions must be made without outside interference.

Reinforcing this view of God's intimacy with man is Edwards' intellectual indebtedness to Petrus van Mastricht, the late seventeenth-century Dutch Reformed theologian steeped in the thought of Francisco Suarez (1548-1617). Suarez, often considered as the greatest scholastic thinker after Thomas Aquinas, had profound influence on the thought of his contemporaries within both Catholic and Protestant circles.

Edwards was also indebted to Francis Turrentin (1623-1687), a Swiss-Italian Protestant theologian inspired by Aquinas as well as by Cardinal Robert Bellarmine (1542-1621). Edwards may not have had direct contact with the writings of St. Thomas, "but given his thorough reading of Turrentin, he may have gone fairly deeply into the heart of Thomistic theology without so realizing. Turrentin functioned as a hermeneutical funnel though which Edwards received the concerns of soteriology."[109]

Ultimately, what Edwards presented to pre-Revolutionary America, as Johnson expressively describes, was a remarkable framework for life "in which the free will, good works, purity of conduct, the appreciation of God's world and the enjoyment of its beauties, and the eventual attainment of salvation, all fitted, blended and fused together by the informing and vivifying energy of love."[110]

What should be understood here — no doubt difficult for the rationalist —is the genuinely spiritual dimension of the Awakening. The revivalists and their followers truly believed in the Holy Spirit. It is He, the third person of the Trinity, who dwells in the soul in grace. It is He who inspires the person to the love of God and to understand the work of salvation in Christ. The revivalists themselves, and those who came to a conversion experience through them, had a theocentric view of life. For them, the Holy Spirit was the prime actor in the great revivals; they were merely His disciples.

George Whitefield

Others revivalists, such as George Whitefield (1714-1770), were soon to follow Edwards, laying the groundwork for democratic concepts such as egalitarianism and religious freedom in the period of the American Revolution. Whitefield, for example, claimed "liberty of conscience to be an 'inalienable right of every rational creature,'" and his supporters in Philadelphia erected a large, new town hall that could be used as a pulpit by anyone of any belief.[111]

Whitefield "may have been the best-known Protestant in the whole world during the eighteenth century."[112] A Calvinist who confessed he never read anything Calvin wrote, ("My doctrines I get from Christ and His apostles: I was taught them by God."), he became the most-recognized religious leader in America in the eighteenth century.

The evidence is that, even after 1740, Whitefield only occasionally grappled with Calvin. In a letter dated February 20, 1741, he writes of having sent for several of Calvin's books, but speaks dismissively about his influence. He states, "You remember what I have often told you about Calvin— but what is Calvin, or what is Luther? Let us look above names and parties; let JESUS, the ever-loving, the ever-lovely JESUS, be our all in all. I embrace the calvinistical scheme, not because Calvin, but JESUS CHRIST, I think, has taught it to me."[113]

Ordained a minister of the Church of England, Whitefield was casual in the extreme about denominational differences, preaching in a more democratic and popular style which no doubt contributed to his wide popularity. During his thirty-three year career, it is estimated he preached 15,000 times in America and Britain.[114]

Whitefield made several trips to America on speaking tours, typically preaching *ex tempore*, directly without notes and relying on the force of his message and charisma. His tour of New England in 1740 drew crowds of up to 8,000 people nearly every day for more than a month. Whitefield's message of God's grace for guilty sinners evoked countless heartfelt conversions and proved to be a key in New England's Great Awakening.

John Witherspoon

Many Congregational, Presbyterian and Baptist pulpits became rallying points for patriotism during the American War for Independence. Only one Protestant minister, however, John Witherspoon, went on to become a signer of the Declaration of Independence and a long-serving member of Congress.[115]

At a time when many Americans seem ambivalent about the linkage of faith and virtue to public life and categorically supportive of Church/state separation, the example of John Witherspoon is of special interest. Witherspoon, a native of Scotland, was born in 1723 to the Reverend James Witherspoon, a Presbyterian pastor, and Anne Walker, a minister's daughter. He was reading the Bible at the age of four, and could soon recite large portions of the New Testament.

Destined for the pulpit, Witherspoon became a confirmed Calvinist and a Presbyterian minister. Unlike some of his peers, who thoughtlessly linked the Bible with political issues, he appealed to conscience and common sense, convinced that God's moral law—*natural law* — was stamped on every man's heart. He made character the touchstone of religious truth and a requisite for effective public service.

Witherspoon's reputation as a leading Evangelical and conciliator caught the attention of American Presbyterians, in search for a new president at the College of New Jersey, later Princeton. Witherspoon accepted the post, and with his wife and five children, arrived at Princeton on August 7, 1768. He was soon absorbed in administration, preaching and teaching.

Witherspoon's tenure as president of Princeton was a long one; he served from 1768 to 1794. Among his students were to come thirty-seven judges, three of whom were appointed to the U.S. Supreme Court, ten cabinet officers, twenty-eight U.S. Senators and forty-nine U. S. Congressmen. Of the fifty-five delegates to the Constitutional Convention, nine were from the College of New Jersey (Princeton), and six graduated while Witherspoon was president.

Witherspoon's house was on the campus of the college and next to it was a Presbyterian church, where he preached regularly. He interacted with his students on a daily basis; historian Garry Wills has called him "probably the most influential teacher in the entire history of American education."[116]

But Witherspoon did not avoid the revolutionary fervor of the times, and the College of New Jersey was to become a hotbed of pro-independence sentiment. By July 1774, he had joined seventy-two representatives of the state to help elect New Jersey delegates to the First Continental Congress. He urged ministers to back the war effort, and a year later was appointed as a representative to the Second Continental Congress and led the movement in New Jersey to depose the royal governor. He was later to serve in Congress from June 1776 to November 1782 and became one of its most influential members and hardest workers.

Two months before the Declaration of Independence, Witherspoon preached a sermon on the political crisis: "The Dominion of Providence Over the Passions of Men." Its purpose was not so much to defend the American cause as to underscore the importance of religious conviction to both personal and public life. "Unless you are united to (Christ) by a lively faith," he told his Princeton congregation, "not the resentment of a haughty monarch, but the sword of divine justice hangs over you."[117]

One of Witherspoon's major arguments in this sermon was that democratic government would ultimately promote religious conviction.

"There is not a single instance in history in which civil liberty was lost, and religious liberty preserved entire."[118] The "Dominion of Providence" sermon was widely distributed and carried the weight of one of the nation's most respected educators and clerics. William Warren Sweet, dean of American Church historians, calls it "one of the most influential utterances during the whole course of the war."[119]

Few argued as strenuously as Witherspoon for the indissoluble link between faith and civic stability. "He is the best friend of America who is most sincere and active in promoting true and undefiled religion," he said, "and who sets himself with the greatest firmness to bear down profanity and immorality of every kind."[120] By "true religion" Witherspoon meant Christianity, but his argumentation was devoid of any denominational bias. He respected the religious pluralism that already existed in the colonies, which is why, on three occasions, Congress turned to him to help author national religious proclamations.

Witherspoon was "a religious conservative concerned with practical public piety." As a Calvinist he insisted on recognizing man's inherent corruption through original sin, and also the possibility of redemption through the operation of God's grace. With Augustine, he believed that the temptation of pride is at the center of man's spiritual challenge.

"What is pride?" asks Augustine in *The City of God*. At bottom, he says, it is "a perverse kind of exaltation" in which one seeks to "abandon the basis on which the mind should be firmly fixed and seeks instead to become self-created, to be like God."[121]

Witherspoon believed that public morals derived from natural law—the law of God is written on men's consciences — but that its ultimate source lay in the public religion of Christianity. Indeed, he felt it would be impossible to maintain public morality or virtue in a citizenry without the underpinnings of an effective religion. In this sense, he saw public morality as distinct from private virtue, but not separate. In fact, public religion was a vital necessity in maintaining public morals.

The Westminster Confession (1646), the founding creedal document of English Calvinism, echoes St. Augustine in its description of mankind's "original corruption" and inclination to evil. For Witherspoon, to not accept this doctrine was to encourage pride and spiritual arrogance by tempting men to forget their moral weakness. More importantly, it cut man off from the possibility of redemption.

John Witherspoon based his life and teaching on the Word of God. "The character of a Christian," he said, "must be taken from Holy Scriptures ... the unerring standard ..."[122] It can be fairly said of him that he devoted his life to instilling the principles of Christianity into the minds and hearts of young men, who then used those principles to shape America.

His young secretary and cousin, John Ramsey Witherspoon, described him as having "the simplicity of a child, the humility of a patriarch and the dignity of a prince."[123] Dr. Roger Schultz of Liberty University said it well: "[John] Adams called him a true son of liberty. So he was. But first, he was a son of the Cross."[124]

The ebbs and tides of religious fervor in America—and a poignant lesson for our own generation —are reflected in the state of religion at Princeton in Witherspoon's later years as president. Once noted for its evangelical fervor, by 1782 it had only two students who professed themselves Christians!

In 1798, the Presbyterian General Assembly, the strongest religious force in that region, described the existing condition of the country this way:

> "We perceive with pain and fearful apprehension a general dereliction of religious principles and practice among our fellow-citizens, a visible and prevailing impiety and contempt for the laws and institutions of religion, and an abounding infidelity, which in many instances tends to atheism itself. The profligacy and corruption of the public morals have advanced with a progress proportionate to our declension in religion. Profaneness, pride, luxury, injustice, intemperance, lewdness, and every species of debauchery and loose indulgence greatly abound."[125]

As for the good news, it could be found in the first rumblings of the Second Great Awakening, taking place at Yale University under its new president Timothy Dwight, grandson of Jonathan Edwards, who became president in 1795. Under Dwight's administration, which met students on their own ground and in frank discussion, the whole moral and religious atmosphere of the college was changed for the better.

Dwight preached a notable series of chapel sermons, for example, on "Theology Explained and Defended" in which he grappled with the issues of deism and materialism. His efforts were admired by his students and a revival began at Yale in 1802, where a third of the student body professed conversion, "to be followed at frequent intervals by other awakenings. Dartmouth, Williams and Amherst Colleges experienced similar religious awakenings, while the movement spread into the middle states and into the South, especially among the Presbyterians."[126]

Chapter Six: Founts of the Founders

John Locke is among "my trinity of the three greatest men the world has ever produced." Thomas Jefferson

I n making the case for an evangelically grounded democracy, it seems appropriate to note the principal founts of religious and philosophical thought for the Founders.

Not surprisingly, the Bible is the clear leader. Based on research covering books, articles, pamphlets and monographs from the period 1760-1805 with explicit political content, the Bible accounted for 34 percent of all citations. No doubt because of the Founders' preoccupation with legal structure, the book of Deuteronomy from the Old Testament, with its heavy emphasis on biblical law, is frequently noted.

On the secular side, the most cited thinkers were Montesquieu, Blackstone and John Locke. Locke most frequently in the early phase of this time frame (1760 to 1780), and Montesquieu and

Blackstone most often in the 1780s and 1790s, when attention was focused on securing the rights won by independence.[127]

Before briefly reviewing these men, a glance at an earlier but highly relevant and influential figure, especially on the thought of John Locke, would seem in order. That man is Richard Hooker.

Richard Hooker

Richard Hooker (1554-1600), was one of the leading Anglican theologians of his time, a man of wide Renaissance learning and one of the greatest English exponents of the doctrine of natural law. Despite his differences with Catholicism, his contemporary, Pope Clement VIII (d.1605) said of Hooker's *A Learned Discourse on Justification*, that it "has in it such seeds of eternity that it will abide until the last fires shall consume all learning."[128]

Perhaps Clement was also thinking of Hooker's great unfinished work, *Of the Laws of Ecclesiastical Polity,* where—using Augustinian language — he says the "reading of scripture is effectual," the sacraments are "necessary" as effectual signs of grace, and the Eucharist is the primary means of sacramental grace. In the Eucharist, Hooker writes, "a creature is exalted above the dignity of all creatures," reflecting his debt to the Greek Fathers, who taught that deification —becoming by grace what God is by nature —is the end result of a faithful sacramental life.[129]

Of the Laws of Ecclesiastical Polity, called by some a masterpiece, has as its philosophical base the works of Aristotle (seen even in his time as "the patriarch of philosophers"), drawing heavily on Aquinas's treatise on Law, which Hooker acknowledged. In *Laws,* Hooker indicates his belief in a Christian commonwealth that operates with the divine and natural law, eternally planted by God in creation, and the human and positive law of reason.

Hooker argued that all positive laws of Church and state are developed from Scriptural revelation, ancient tradition, reason and experience.[130] Holy Writ, is, in fact, a gift of grace that offers both nature and humanity a "more divine perfection."

Hooker believed that all of creation is teleological (from the Greek *telos,* meaning end), such that every created thing has a divinely appointed end or purpose. Law exists, said Hooker, not so much to point out our sins, failures and shortcomings, but to direct us toward the end for which we were made. This view is one of a created order and divine providence; God orders by way of law, and we are never free of these laws.

The key to understanding Hooker's theory of law—and what makes his thought so relevant to modern times that has abandoned the link between belief and culture — is his effort to reconcile faith and reason. The *jus divinum* with the *jus naturae,* the harmony of the natural and the supernatural. Hooker had to balance the scriptural radicalism of the Puritans — their rigid appeal to the Bible and that "Scripture is the only rule to frame our actions by"— with their admission that God has left us "at greater liberty in things civil."[131]

Hooker believed, with Calvin, that reason is not the foundation of revelation but the opposite. Reason reveals that which is hidden or unclear within revelation. This places both within the tradition of "faith seeking understanding" that is so conspicuous in Augustine and Anselm.

John Calvin, in chapter VIII of book I of *The Institutes,* entitled "So Far as Human Reason Goes, Sufficiently Firm Proofs are at Hand to Establish the Credibility of Scripture," affirms that Scripture is "not sustained by external props" such as reason, yet we may use reason to prove the authority of Scripture. As Calvin wrote:

> "Once we have embraced it (the authority of Scripture) devoutly as its dignity deserves, and have recognized it to be above the common sort of things, those arguments (from reason)—not strong enough before to engraft and fix the certainty of scripture in our minds — become very useful aids."[132]

This respect for reason is why wherever Calvinists went, from Transylvania to Massachusetts, they brought with them not only the Bible and Calvin's *Institutes*, but also the Latin grammar and the study of the classics.[133]

It is also interesting to note Calvin's position on the separation of Church and state. He actually suggested that Church and state were "conjoined" (both were divinely ordained, after all), and hoped each would sustain the other in fulfilling their divine obligations. "Calvin's principle of separation of Church and state bore little resemblance ... to the modern American understanding of "a high and impregnable wall between Church and state."[134]

As for Luther, he held that "the temporal government is a divine order" and urged all cities in Germany to establish Christian schools.[135]

Hooker acknowledges that human reason is "darkened by sin", such that we cannot even discern the sinfulness of "gross iniquity."[136] In this situation, the laws of nature remain but reason cannot apprehend them, thus calling for a "more divine perfection"[137] This is the reason why God inspired prophets and apostles to compose the scriptures: "the principal intent of Scripture is to deliver the duties supernatural,"[138] and Holy Writ is a gift of grace that offers both nature and humanity a "more divine perfection."

Hooker's definition of law echoes almost word for word the definition of Thomas Aquinas. Will and command are not to him the constituent elements of law. There is a close connection between law and reason: Law is, as Aquinas has said, *aliquid rationis,* meaning that law is something pertaining to reason.[139]

This is quite different from Luther's discrediting of reason and promoting the primacy of the will. It differs from the nominalism of the Reformation, which destroyed the hierarchical conception of the world and replaced reason with will and its insistence upon Scripture and the revealed law of God as the sole rule of human action. And in so doing, we must add, laid the foundation for the moral relativism and cultural subjectivism endemic to modern times.

As for Church-state relations, Hooker condemns Machiavelli and the "politic use of religion," refusing to accept that the Christian ideal and Christian principles may yield to political necessities. True religion is, for him, both something personal and also a goal for the national consciousness, entirely independent of the competence and power of the state itself. So, while arguing for an appropriate separation of Church and state, Hooker would have no problem with the notion of theocentric humanism.

In a message one wishes would resonate more strongly in our secular times, Hooker believed there should be no anxiety about the condition of religion as long as the national consciousness keeps faith with the main dictates of Christianity. The great English and Christian statesman William Gladstone summarized Hooker's position as expressing "the great doctrine that the State is a person, having a conscience, cognizant of matters of religion, and bound by all constitutional and natural means to advance it."[140]

In his excellent book on medieval political thought, Alexander Passerin D'Entreves writes, "This idea of the dependence of state-power and state-action on higher and indeed eternal values is not so much a legacy of medieval as of Christian political thought. To reject it can only mean to renounce Christianity altogether, and to raise the state or the tribe to the place which the Christian reserves for God alone." [141]

Izaak Walton, Hooker's biographer, quotes King James I as saying, "I observe there is in Mr. Hooker no affected language; but a grave, comprehensive, clear manifestation of reason, and that backed with the authority of the scriptures, the fathers and schoolmen, and with all law both sacred and civil."[142]

Locke, Hooker's intellectual protégé, never questioned the role of religion in inspiring the rule of law. He wrote: "Laws human must be made according to the general laws of Nature, and without contradiction to any positive law of Scripture, otherwise they are ill made."[143]

Locke strongly believed in the natural rights of man; that they were set in nature by God and that they have validity everywhere. "The law of Nature stands as an eternal rule to all men, legislators as well as others. The rule that they make for other men's actions must ... be conformable to the Law of Nature, i.e., to the will of God."[144]

John Locke

If largely unknown today, John Locke remains one of the most defining names in American history and a key link to its evangelical roots. This English philosopher (1632-1704), was a devout Protestant who wrote extensively on religion, and his political writings were exceptionally influential in bringing about the American Revolution. Often called the father of classical liberalism, Locke is the thinker who had the deepest intellectual influence on our Founders.

Locke was by far the single most frequently-cited political philosopher in the years 1760 to 1776, the period leading up to the Declaration of Independence. John Adams praised Locke's *Essay on Human Understanding,* openly acknowledging that "Mr. Locke ... has steered his course into the unenlightened regions of the human mind, and like Columbus, has discovered a new world."[145]

Declaration signer Benjamin Rush, also a founder of the Bible Society of Philadelphia and a supporter of Christianity in public life and in education, said that Locke was "a justly celebrated oracle" as to the principles ... of government. Benjamin Franklin said that Locke was one of the "Best English authors" for the study of "history, rhetoric, logic, moral and natural philosophy."

James Wilson, a signer of the Declaration of Independence and the Constitution and an original Justice of the Supreme Court, said that for the doctrine of toleration in matters of religion, "the world has been thought to owe much to the inestimable writings of the celebrated Locke."

Far from being a deist, Wilson called Locke "—one of the most able, most sincere and most amiable assertors of Christianity and true philosophy,"— noting that his writings "have been perverted to purposes, which he would have deprecated and prevented had he discovered or foreseen them."[146]

Thomas Jefferson went so far as to say that Locke was among "my trinity of the three greatest men the world has ever produced."

[147] And John Quincy Adams once wrote that "the Declaration of Independence (was)—founded upon one and the same theory of government—expounded in the writings of Locke."[148]

Locke's influence did not end with the Founders and our earliest years.

• In 1833, for example, Justice Story, author of the famed *Commentaries on the Constitution,* described Locke as "a most strenuous asserter of liberty: who helped establish in this country the sovereignty of the people over the government, majority rule with minority protection, and the *rights of conscience."* (emphasis added). [149]

It's worthy of note, in the context of the natural law argument of this book, that Justice Story, in the celebrated case relative to slave trade in 1822, *La Jeune Eugenie,* argued that the law may not incorporate what is by nature wrong, saying: "(the trade in slaves) is repugnant to the great principles of Christian duty, the dictates of natural religion, the obligations of good faith and morality, and the eternal maxims of social justice."

In contrast, two years later, in the case of *The Antelope,* Chief Justice Marshall wrote "that slavery is contrary to the law of nature will scarcely be denied," and then, unfortunately acquiescing to legal positivism, suggested that this 'wrongness' was rooted, not in natural law but in international law.

The gravity of such moral relativism is reflected in Marshall's conclusion that therefore "this (slave) trade, in which all have participated, must remain lawful to those who cannot be induced to relinquish it" and that therefore "this traffic remains lawful to those whose government have not forbidden it." A classic case, indeed, for moral relativity!

• In 1834, George Bancroft, called the "Father of American History," described Locke as "the rival of the 'ancient philosophers' to whom the world has 'erected statues,'" and noted that Locke esteemed the pursuit of truth the first object of life and ... "never sacrificed a conviction to an interest."[150]

• In 1872, historian Richard Frothingham said that Locke's principles —principles that he said were "inspired and imbued with the Christian idea of man"—produced the "leading principles of republicanism" that was "summed up in the Declaration of Independence and became the American theory of government."[151]

• And in the 1890s, the celebrated nineteenth-century historian John Fiske, said that Locke brought "the idea of complete liberty of conscience in matters of religion" to America, allowing persons with "any sort of notion about God" to be protected "against all interference or molestation," and that Locke should "be ranked in the same order as Aristotle."[152]

In more recent times, Locke has even received presidential recognition.

• President Ronald Reagan confirmed that much in America "testifies to the power and the vision of free men inspired by the ideals and dedication to liberty of John Locke ..."[153]

• President Bill Clinton reminded the British Prime Minister that "throughout our history our peoples have reinforced each other in the living classroom of democracy. It is difficult to imagine Jefferson, for example, without John Locke before him."[154]

The point of emphasizing Locke here of course is twofold. The first is the extraordinary influence his thought had, not only on the writings of the Founders but also on men of serious purpose and civil concern for generations in this country. As importantly, given the foundational ideas he represented, Locke's thought had an exceptionally long reach, both historically and philosophically, back to the foremost thinkers of the Western Christian tradition and the roots of democracy.

As a notable example, Locke was aware of and supportive of the natural rights theory of Thomas Aquinas, the most renowned Christian advocate of natural law theory. As is well known, Aquinas's thought in turn was indebted to the metaphysics of the illustrious Greek philosopher, Aristotle (384-322 BC).

Some of the Founders — most notably John Adams and James Wilson —refer frequently to Aristotle and show a deep familiarity with his *Politics*. Indeed Aristotle —who might be called the 'first father' of natural law political theory—seems to have enjoyed an authority among the Founders not unlike that which he exercised over the learned world for centuries.

A passage from Wilson's treatise, *Of the General Principles of Law and Obligation*, is illustrative: "Why should a few received authors stand up like Hercules's columns, beyond which there should be no sailing or discovery? To Aristotle, more than to any other writer either ancient or modern, this expostulation is strictly applicable. Hear what the learned Grotius (1583-1645) says on this subject: 'Among philosophers, Aristotle deservedly holds the chief place, whether you consider his method of treating subjects, or the acuteness of his distinctions, or the weight of his reasons.'"[155]

As for the famous Dutch lawyer, theologian and statesman, whose two great works are *The Rights of War and Peace* and *The Truth of the Christian Religion,* Hugo Grotius's main academic purpose was to apply Christian principles to the world of politics. His writings were highly respected by the founding fathers and were standard studies in American colonial colleges.

James Madison called Grotius, "the father of the modern code of Nations."[156] Hamilton wrote of him, "Apply yourself, without delay, to the study of the law of nature. I would recommend to you Grotius, Pufendorf, Locke."

When asked once what was the philosophy underlying the Declaration of Independence, Jefferson replied that: "All its authority rests ... on the harmonizing sentiments of the day, whether expressed in conversation, in letters, printed essays, or in the elementary books of public right, as Aristotle, Cicero, Locke, Sidney, etc."[157]

John Adams similarly wrote that the principles of the American Revolution "are the principles of Aristotle and Plato, of Livy and Cicero, and Sidney, Harrington, and Locke; the principles of nature and eternal reason; the principles on which the whole government over us now stands."[158] Adams also wrote of Aristotle: "Aristotle says that a 'government where the laws alone should prevail, would be the kingdom of God.' This indeed shows that this great philosopher had much admiration for such a government."[159]

Montesquieu

In the era of American constitution-making, no political writer was more often cited and none was thought to be of greater authority than Charles-Louis de Secondat, baron de La Brède et de Montesquieu (1689-1755), generally referred to as simply Montesquieu.

Montesquieu was a French social commentator and political thinker who lived during the Enlightenment. Montesquieu is famous for his articulation of the theory of separation of powers, which is taken for granted in modern discussions of government and implemented in many constitutions. Montesquieu's magnum opus, *The Spirit of Laws*, was translated into English, Italian, German, Latin, Danish, Dutch, Polish and Russian, and appeared in more than 160 editions.

In *The Federalist*, James Madison called Montesquieu an "oracle," and both Madison and Alexander spoke of him as "the celebrated Montesquieu." Montesquieu is a particularly interesting figure here in that he was a French Roman Catholic who wrote vigorously against the Church early in his career (*The Persian Laws*), and then drastically changed his views thirty years later, when he wrote *The Spirit of the Laws*. In this book, which became the political bible of learned men of the times, he devotes several chapters to how religion applies in political scenarios.

He advanced the utilitarian opinion that any sort of religion is appropriate for enforcing a state's power and stability. The slight overlap between them helps ensure the state's survival. "Without religion ('the Christian religion is a stranger to mere despotic power') man is without morals and lacks appropriate judgment; the social construct of religion ... keeps them at bay from wreaking havoc across the universe."[160]

The Spirit of the Laws deals with the external effects of religion and how government and religion should interact. Here Montesquieu proposes yet another idea— that of religious tolerance for all religions equally to avoid a vicious chain of religion oppressing religion. However innocuous this sounds in contemporary society, it was a strikingly countercultural statement by Montesquieu; he was advocating religious freedom and equality at a time when most monarchs chose how, when, and where their subjects worshiped. Montesquieu also puts forth the modern idea behind the separation of Church and state.

Far from thinking that there can be a conflict between religion and society, Montesquieu insists that the one is useful to the other. "Something," he says, "must be fixed and permanent, and religion is that something." He says again, more clearly: "What a wonderful thing is the Christian religion! It seems to aim only at happiness in a future life, and yet it secures our happiness in this life also." He does not dream of separating Church and state, nor of subjecting the former to the latter: "I have never claimed that the interests of religion should give way to those of the State, but that they should go hand in hand."[161]

As for separation of powers, Montesquieu's view is that concentration of legislative, executive and judicial functions either in one single person or a body of persons results in abuse of authority. He believed government should be so organized that each should be entrusted to different persons or branches, each performing distinct functions within the sphere of power assigned to it.

The early American statesmen were very familiar with "De l'esprit des lois" and from it derived much of their idea of federal government. Jefferson, Hamilton, Madison and Jay, who wrote in the Federalist Papers in defense of the new Constitution, were all enthusiastic readers of Montesquieu. Such attention ensured a universal reputation for Montesquieu, which he peacefully enjoyed until his death, which he prepared for by receiving the sacraments of the Church, and showing every outward mark of perfect obedience to her laws.[162]

In Montesquieu we see yet again the influence of a highly revered political writer on the authors of the Constitution. Montesquieu thoroughly embraced the link between the inspiration of the Gospel and the political freedoms making their appearance in the fledgling democracy of America. Indeed, as he wrote, they are both best served by going "hand in hand."[163]

Chapter Seven: Conscience, Natural Law and Religious Liberty

John Henry Cardinal Newman, who reflected deeply and wrote incisively on the subject, says of conscience that it is "the aboriginal Vicar of Christ."

Since freedom of conscience is at the heart of this discussion, some relevant thoughts on the notion of conscience, both from our Founders and from our best thinkers both past and present, would seem appropriate.

First let us acknowledge—as did our Founders—that for all its importance to personal dignity, conscience is not the supreme court of appeal to decide, categorically and infallibly, what is good and what is evil. Conscience is a manifestation of God in the human person. It is, as it were, a law of God. But it is not God.

Not to recognize this reality is to make conscience something that it cannot be, namely *the creator* of the moral order and moral law.

Conscience does not answer only to itself; to make it so is to submit to a valueless subjectivism or a hopeless idealism. We must recognize that freedom of conscience enables it, rightly so, to recognize and submit to a higher law. The Founders understood this, which is why they strongly embraced the notion of natural law, so well explicated over the centuries by the great minds of Western civilization.

What they understood is that the natural law, coming from above (its objective dimension) but written into the hearts of all men (its subjective dimension), provides the measure of the conscience, not vice versa. Hence human reason, for which the Founders had the greatest respect, is, in a certain sense, autonomous. It is not meant to be coerced. It must be free. At the same time, while it sheds light on moral behavior, it is not the cause of moral behavior, as shall be explored.

Both reason and the moral law, as our great men and traditions teach us, participate in and are subject to a higher law, namely to God's wisdom and to eternal law. Divine authority alone, manifested both in an evangelical and an ontological way, is the basis for an absolute moral obligation and the sanctions that human behavior entails. John Henry Cardinal Newman, who reflected deeply and wrote incisively on the subject, says of conscience that it is "the aboriginal Vicar of Christ."

In his *Certain Difficulties Felt by Anglicans in Catholic Teaching,* Newman writes: "Conscience is a law of the mind; yet (Christians) would not grant that it is nothing more; I mean that it was not a dictate, nor conveyed the notion of responsibility, of duty, of a threat and a promise— (Conscience) is a messenger of him, who, both in nature and in grace speaks to us behind a veil, and teaches and rules us by his representatives."[164]

For Newman, and for many other seminal thinkers, conscience is at the very heart of the human person. As the great Vatican II document *Gaudium et Spes* puts it: "Conscience is man's most secret core, and his sanctuary. There he is alone with God, whose voice echoes in his depths."[165]

Thus it is important for every person to be sufficiently present to himself —not so easy in modern times — so as to hear and to follow the voice of his conscience. This interiority is all the more necessary as life distracts from any reflection, self-examination or introspection. As St. Augustine writes: "Return to your conscience, question it— turn inward, brethren, and in everything you do, see God as your witness."[166]

The greatest of the Aristotelians, St. Thomas Aquinas, brought his notion of 'tabula rasa' (clean tablet) to the forefront of Christian thought in the thirteenth century. His realism sharply contrasted with the previously held and deeply influential Platonic notion of innate ideas—the discovery of reality *within* thought —which led to a long philosophical trajectory of subjectivism, determinism and idealism.

For Plato, when we behold some phenomena of the real world, the mind —*the tablet* —is moved to remember via intuition the Idea which it had formerly contemplated in the higher world. This contrasted sharply with the thought of Aristotle, who understood knowing as the process of abstracting ideas from existing things, from *reality*. That process, then, while driven from within in order to conceptualize and 'write' on the blank tablet, is dependent on that which is without, namely *the real world*.

The writings of Aquinas on the *tabula rasa* theory stood unprogressed for several centuries. A key reason for mentioning it here is that the modern idea of the tabula rasa resurfaces in John Locke's *An Essay Concerning Human Understanding*. As understood by Locke, tabula rasa meant, as with Aristotle, that the mind of the individual was born 'blank' (the soul begins without shape or intellectual imprint) and must 'open up' to reality.

An important aspect of this reality for the human person is precisely the notion of conscience, which is, as it were, embedded in human nature. Which is to say it comes from without—(its objective dimension) — not from within the human subject. Conscience has, however, a vitally important subjective dimension as well. If its objective side speaks to the truth of an action — 'do this, avoid that'—its subjective side lies in the subject's use of freedom; namely to actually "do this action, or avoid that action."

This is contrary to Lutheran *immanentism*, a modern myth whereby truth and life must be sought only *within* the human self. Everything extrinsic to the subject, (i.e., that which comes from without or is "other"), is a crime against the spirit and against sincerity. Everything extrinsic to us—that does not come from 'the self' —can only lead to the destruction and death of the self.

This, of course, is not what conscience is all about. Conscience is a law man discovers within himself, not one that he lays upon himself. It is a law inscribed by God that presents to man the highest norms of human life —eternal, objective and universal—freely obliging him to discover and assent to these norms in order to live out his dignity and reach true human maturity.

Conscience is the way to authentic development, both personal and social, and to love. "By conscience, in a wonderful way, that law is made known which is fulfilled in the love of God and of one's neighbor." (Cf. Mt. 22: 37-40; Gal. 5:14) "Through loyalty to conscience Christians are joined to other men in the search for truth and for the right solution to so many moral problems which arise both in the life of individuals and from social relationships."[167]

Thus the inner freedom —the *conscience* of the individual —must in all cases be protected. And for a truly sublime reason, namely that in a very real way each individual (better said, *each person*, guided by grace), is the author of his own soul. That is, he gives his own soul not only intellectual imprint but— via virtuous action— shape and character. He does this by prudently forming judgments of conscience that are both sincere and true, and by acting accordingly.

In Aristotelian terms, we can say that, given his power to make choices of good or bad, the person is the "efficient cause" of his own personality. As Karol Wojtyla (now St. John Paul II) put it, for all of the nobility of the human intellect, self-determination takes place through *acts of the will*, through this central power of the human soul. "The will is the person's power of self-determination."[168]

This remarkable capability of 'personal authorship' —for which the Founders had a profound intuition —must always be protected because it is of the essence of human freedom and authentic personhood. It is a reflection of God himself—and must not be denied.

The Catholic Church has given great thought to the notion of conscience and exerted much energy in its defense. So it is of interest to briefly review a relatively recent statement on how the Church sees this defining dimension of the human personality. Conscience appears in the Church's Vatican II document *The Constitution on the Church in the Modern World (Gaudium et Spes)*, Chapter 1, on the "Dignity of the Human Person."

"In the depths of his conscience, man detects a law which he does not impose upon himself, but which holds him to obedience. Always summoning him to love good and avoid evil, the voice of conscience when necessary speaks to his heart: do this, shun that. For man has in his heart a law written by God; to obey it is the very dignity of man; according to it he will be judged. Conscience is the most secret core and sanctuary of a man. There he is alone with God, Whose voice echoes in his depths.

"In a wonderful manner conscience reveals that law which is fulfilled by love of God and neighbor. In fidelity to conscience, Christians are joined with the rest of men in the search for truth, and for the genuine solution to the numerous problems which arise in the life of individuals from social relationships.

"Hence the more right conscience holds sway, the more persons and groups turn aside from blind choice and strive to be guided by objective norms of morality. Conscience frequently errs from invincible ignorance without losing its dignity. The same cannot be said for a man who cares but little for truth and goodness, or for a conscience which by degrees grows practically sightless as a result of habitual sin.

"Only in freedom can man direct himself toward goodness. Our contemporaries make much of this freedom and pursue it eagerly; and rightly to be sure. Often, however, they foster it perversely as a license for doing whatever pleases them, even if it is evil. For its part, *authentic freedom is an exceptional sign of the divine image within man.* For God has willed that man remain "under control of his own decisions," so that he can seek his Creator spontaneously, and come to utter and blissful perfection through loyalty to Him." [169]

Natural Law

We see then, as did such notable Protestant theologians as Jonathan Edwards and Richard Hooker, that man's supreme dignity is both to participate in the divine nature and be destined toward it. Thus, each individual must be free to both intellectually understand and to willfully shape the content of his or her character, i.e., willfully follow his conscience (or not) in responding to a higher law within. Hence the imperative need for freedom of conscience. Lacking this freedom, man simply cannot fulfill himself.

At the same time, it must be said that man's basic identity or nature as a member of the human species can be violated, but it cannot be altered. It is from this presumption of a free, self-authored mind, combined with an immutable human nature that explicitly manifests God's will, that the Lockean doctrine of "natural" rights" derives.

At least part of the link between Aquinas, the greatest of the Scholastics (Schoolmen) and writing in the thirteenth century, and the empiricist Locke, writing in the seventeenth, rests on the issue of natural law, which was given extensive review by both men. "Locke ... was familiar with the great medieval tradition of politics to which modern liberty owes so much: the tradition that government emanates from the community, is subordinate to law, and must seek the popular welfare. He had learned this doctrine from his reading of Richard Hooker," an Anglican theologian with a deep historical sense, sometimes called the English Aquinas.[170]

Carl L. Becker, a renowned student of the religious philosophy underlying the Declaration of Independence, wrote the classic study on this subject. Becker is perhaps best known for "The Heavenly City of the Eighteenth-Century Philosophers,'[171] four lectures on The Enlightenment delivered at Yale University. His assertion—that the 'philosophes' in the "Age of Reason" relied far more upon Christian assumptions than they cared to admit—has been influential despite being attacked, no doubt in part because of passages like this:

> "In the thirteenth century the key words would no doubt be God, sin, grace, salvation, heaven and the like; in the nineteenth century, matter, fact, matter-of-fact, evolution, progress; in the twentieth century, relativity, process, adjustment, function, complex. In the eighteenth century the words without which no enlightened person could reach a restful conclusion were nature, natural law, first cause, reason, sentiment, humanity, perfectibility."

By the twentieth century, there is little to be found in political discourse referencing God, or metaphysical concepts of any sort. What we could find in recent presidential elections are words such as change, economy, energy, taxes, jobs, health care, immigration, etc. When what we call moral issues: marriage, abortion, contraception, and even education— which has a definite moral dimension —did make it to center stage, they were typically treated as 'behavioral,' not moral issues.

In denial of their moral dimension, these 'behavior issues,' in these modern times, are typically determined in the public arena by personal choice and majority vote; 'i.e. does it 'feel good,' and 'do they love one another,' or by judicial *dikat*, rather than by any binding standards of 'right and wrong.'

Whatever the contemporary amnesia on the subject, the good news about natural law is that it may be disputed or ignored, but it cannot, rationally, be refuted. Rationality is one of its constituents. Nor is it going away, so let us look at what Aquinas has to say on the subject. Characteristically, he notes three distinct meanings of the word 'natural.' The third of these, from the classical world, he defined as "an inclination in man to the good, according to the rational nature which is proper to him. As, for example, man has a natural inclination to know the truth about God, and to live in society."

This 'natural law,' as a natural inclination (that is, *within* the being of things and preceding all formulation), was discoverable by right reason. In the medieval hierarchy, natural law was subordinate to the highest of all laws, namely the Eternal Law, which comprehended all others. The Eternal Law was the full mind of God, of which something, but not all, could be known to man. Part of this law had been revealed in the Bible, or communicated through the Church (Positive Divine Law), and part of it could be discovered by human reason (Natural Law). [172]

The idea of natural law goes much further than Aquinas. It extends all the way back to St. Augustine and the Church Fathers and to St. Paul, as when Paul says, "When the Gentiles who have not the Law, do by nature the things contained in the Law, these, having not the Law, are a law unto themselves ..." (Romans 2:14). And as Jacques Maritain points out, it goes back even further; to the Stoics, to Cicero, and to the great moralists and poets of antiquity, particularly Sophocles (496-406 BC).

Sophocles's Antigone, for example, "is aware that in transgressing the human law and being crushed by it she was obeying a better commandment, the unwritten and unchangeable laws ..." "She is the eternal heroine of natural law for, as she puts it, they were not, those unwritten laws, born out of today's or yesterday's sweet will, 'but they live always and forever, and no man knows from where they have arisen.'"[173]

The point here, of course, is that natural law is "transcendent" of both time and place. Which means not only that it is ageless, but also—however much it may be transgressed or ignored— it is above historical vicissitudes. However much it is disobeyed, in the form of right conscience it is always there to guide and to serve.

Augustine on Natural Law

St. Augustine makes frequent reference to natural law, especially in his *Confessions*. In many instances, he sees it as the eternal law made manifest in man, or as St. Thomas put it, "The natural law is the eternal law from the perspective of the rational creature."[174]

In his *On Eighty Three Diverse Questions*, Augustine describes it this way: "from this ineffable and sublime arrangement of affairs, then, which is accomplished by divine providence, a natural law (*naturalis lex*) is, so to speak, inscribed upon the rational soul, so that in the very living out of this life and in their earthly activities people might hold to the tenor of such dispositions."

The great medieval historian, Etienne Gilson, expands on this notion of natural law in his book, *The Christian Philosophy of Saint Augustine*:

> "There is a law in God which, in Him, is simply God Himself, and to this law everything which is not God is subject. We call it the eternal law ... This immutable law illumines our conscience as the divine light enlightens our understanding

... There is therefore a kind of law in us also, consisting of the imperative commands of conscience; its rules are so many primary certitudes. We call it the natural law. It derives its certitude from the fact that it is simply a kind of transcript in our souls of the eternal law subsisting immutably in God. Consequently, all the detailed commands of our moral conscience, all the changing acts of legislation governing peoples spring from one and the same law."[175]

John Courtney Murray

Fr. John Courtney Murray, S.J. provides an incisive contemporary perspective on the relevance of natural law to good governance. It's unusual for a Catholic priest to appear on the cover of *Time* magazine, but it has happened. Fr. Murray's distinguished features graced the cover of *Time's* December 12, 1960, issue.

The cover story was titled "U.S. Catholics and the State." The occasion was the appearance of Murray's book *We Hold These Truths: Catholic Reflections on the American Proposition,* written as a Catholic president was about to direct the course of American public life for the first time.

Over the previous decade, Murray had written thirteen essays exploring the correlation between America's public beliefs and Catholic philosophy and theology. Using lucid prose and a distinguished level of reason and rhetoric, Murray studied the civic consensus whereby a people acquired its identity and sense of purpose and becomes a nation.

Not surprisingly, Murray was an orthodox proponent of the natural law tradition of Aristotle and Thomas Aquinas. He was convinced

Catholic thought could illuminate the spiritual goods that our Founders had discovered about political life, but which had a deeper tradition than they realized. Murray argued that it was this richer theoretical foundation— rooted in Christian and Catholic thought— that is greatly needed in modern times to defend our constitution and our freedoms.

Murray concurred with the founding fathers that there exists in America a body of substantive truths that "command the structure and the courses of the political-economic system of the United States." At its foundation, this consensus affirmed a free people under a limited government, guided by law and ultimately resting on the sovereignty of God.

Unfortunately, says Murray, this consensus has long eroded. In no small part, he says, this is because "the American university long since bade a quiet goodbye to the whole notion of an American consensus," implying that there are no truths we hold in common and no natural law that structures our moral universe and binds us to it in a common obedience.[176]

Rejecting both Liberal individualism and Marxist collectivism, Murray's solution was to stress the prevailing validity of natural law in a new age, "its secure anchorage in the order of reality." He wrote, "The doctrine of natural law offers a more profound metaphysic, and more integral humanism, a fuller rationality, a more complete philosophy of man in his nature and history." Beyond all that, it also "furnishes the basis for a firmer faith and a more tranquil, because more reasoned, hope in the future."[177]

"We hold these truths to be self-evident ..." So begins the preamble of the Declaration of Independence. These truths, based on principles and doctrines that are both classic and Christian in origin, helped establish the identity of a people, both for itself and within the community of nations. They were laboriously wrought out of centuries of thought, of experience, of wars and of suffering, and of people struggling to live freely and peacefully among one another.

And so Murray asks: What are these truths, and why do we hold them? We hold them first, he says, because they are a patrimony. "They are a heritage from history, through whose dark and bloody pages there runs like a silver thread the tradition of civility. This is the first reason why the consensus continually calls for public argument. The consensus is an intellectual heritage; it may be lost to mind or deformed in the mind. Its final depository is the public mind. This is indeed a perilous place to deposit what ought to be kept safe ..."[178]

This perilousness of place is the reason why the argument must be preserved, says Murray. So that we don't forget, so that we don't become skeptical, so that we don't succumb to the "predatory moths of deceitful doxia"—erroneous public opinion, dubious rhetoric and noxious philosophizing.

More importantly, Murray reminds us, we hold these truths *because they are true*:

> "They have been found in the structure of reality by that dialectic of observation and reflection that is called philosophy. But as the achievement of reason and experience the consensus again presents itself for argument. Its vitality depends on a constant scrutiny of political experience ...

> "On both of these titles, as a heritage and as a public philosophy, the American consensus needs to be constantly argued. If the public argument dies from disinterest, or

> subsides into the angry mutterings of polemic, or rises to the shrillness of hysteria, or trails off into positivistic triviality, or gets lost in a morass of semantics, you may be sure that the barbarian is at the gates of the City."[179]

And who are the barbarians? Well, says Murray, they needn't be dressed in bearskin. They might be wearing a Brooks Brothers suit or even an academic gown, but are, nonetheless "untutored in the high tradition of civility" who reject reasonable conversation according to reasonable laws. Indeed, they may even hold high political office.

Or as Murray would put it: "Today the barbarian is the man who makes open and explicit rejection of the traditional role of reason and logic in human affairs. He is the man who reduces all spiritual and moral questions to the test of practical results or to an analysis of language or to decision in terms of individual subjective feeling."[180]

Russell Kirk chillingly summed up the diminution of reason and respect for morality in public affairs this way: "liberalism is expiring before our very eyes for lack of the higher imagination."[181]

Immanuel Kant

As a contemporary of the Founders and witness to the developing years of the American republic, and because of his philosophical repute, the thought of Immanuel Kant bears some reflection here.

Immanuel Kant (1724-1804) was a classic liberal and one of Western philosophy's most influential thinkers. His life corresponded with the founding of the United States, though his political writing came after the American Revolution, which he favored, and also the French Revolution in its earlier, less violent stages.

As did Jefferson, Kant claimed that there are principles common to all humanity: the principles of morality, of the republican constitution, and of the ethical state, which serve as criteria to evaluate personal maxims and political institutions.

For example Kant wrote, "the idea of a constitution in harmony with the natural right of human beings, one namely in which the citizens obedient to the law, besides being united, ought also to be legislative, lies at the basis of all political form."[182]

As for law itself, Kant put it this way: "A law has to carry with it an absolute necessity if it is to be valid morally—valid, that is, as a ground of obligation."[183] For that reason, he said, laws had to be categorical, "otherwise they would not be laws."[184]

Kant's parents were devoted followers of the Pietist branch of the Lutheran Church, believing that religion belongs to the inner life expressed in simplicity and obedience to the moral law. Kant's tomb at the Konigsberg cathedral is inscribed in German, saying, "The starry heavens above me and the moral law within me," the two things that he declared at the conclusion of his second *Critique*.

Kant is considered, at least by some, as a direct offspring of the Middle Ages.[185] Kant quotes the Bible, he develops the proof of the existence of God from final causes, and he is fond of repeating the Hebrew meaning of his name Immanuel — *God with us*. In religion, Kant is a supporter of the Christian doctrine. He advocates the existence of free will; when he undertakes his *Critique of Pure Reason*, he is morally certain of the existence of God and of another life.

He expresses the final conclusion he reaches in Christian terms, denouncing, as believers do, the insufficiency of speculative reason and ending with an act of faith. In a word, says German philosopher Friedrich Paulsen, Kant's work is an apologetic and may be compared to St. Thomas's *Summa Contra Gentiles*.[186]

Kant's *Critique of Pure Reason* (1781) argues for optimizing the freedom of the body politic as the best way to maximize justice and public virtue. In ethics Kant was an extreme rationalist to the point of idealism, maintaining that moral principles are objectively valid commands of the *a priori* reason. An action, according to him, has moral worth only if it is done from a sense of duty and never because it has been inspired by utilitarian considerations.

By the time of the Enlightenment, there was a dissolution of the close link between nature and reason as the basis of natural law, and Kant is a leading proponent of this understanding. His major work, *The Metaphysics of Morals* (1797), makes extensive use of natural law, but in the normative sense now understood as a subjective *law of reason*, rather than a law *written on the heart*.

Kant's philosophy has been criticized on numerous counts, including his sympathy to Luther's revolt in theology, to Descartes's revolt in philosophy, and to Rousseau's revolt in ethics. Kant's resulting "subjectivistic transcendentalism," as it has been called, was not a part of the great American experiment in democracy and has been largely rejected today.

But his ethical thought still has relevance to the metaphysics of the life issues: abortion, euthanasia, etc. He wrote, for example, "Suicide is not permitted under any condition. Man has, in his own person, a thing inviolable; it is something holy that has been entrusted to us."[187]

Locke agreed with this view of the sacredness of life for the same reason: "Though Man in the State of Nature have an uncontrollable Liberty, to dispose of his Person or Possessions, yet he has not Liberty to destroy himself, or so much as any Creature in his Possession— there cannot be supposed any such Subordination among us, that may Authorize us to destroy one another, as if we were made for one another's uses, as the inferior ranks of Creatures are for ours."[188]

Despite Locke's considerable influence on America, perhaps he remains so forgotten today precisely because he was so profoundly religious. In Locke's first treatise, for example, he invoked the Bible in at least 1,349 references, and, in his second, 157 times.

Locke's last major work in 1695 was entitled *The Reasonableness of Christianity*, wherein he wrote, "Where was there any such Code that Mankind might have recourse to, as their unerring Rule, before our Savior's time?"[189] The identity of this Savior and his influence were not lost on John Adams and other Founders.

It's relevant to note here that the natural law to which Locke refers, combined with the ideal of charity, is the fundamental ideal of the moral philosophy of Thomas Aquinas. Most importantly, it points the way beyond the raw legalism and selfish secularism of modernity to a dynamic *theocentric* humanism able to reconstruct the evangelical vision of the Founders.

For example, in the Thomistic ethic "charity"—the principal of the theological virtues and of divine origin (and an often forgotten element in political life today) —carries an even weightier significance than the concept of natural law, in no small part because charity, as a grace, is of higher origin.

This was Hooker's observation as well. Namely, that the object of human laws is and can only be outward action; laws have no control over thoughts and feelings. Hooker thus throws light on the vital difference between legal conformity, the moral value of action, and the need to distinguish between the two. In so doing, he also clarifies the impossibility of establishing a compassionate and caring nation only through the instruments of law.

A civilization of love —the very purpose of freedom —must be created, indeed *inspired,* by its citizenry. It cannot be juridically mandated.

The law unto itself is insufficient; it must be lived properly to be effective. Thomistic moral philosophy, centered on the habit and virtue of charity, is also the basis for Jacques Maritain's understanding of religion and the political order. Maritain writes:

> "The important thing for the political life of the world and for the resolution of the crisis of civilization ... is to affirm that democracy is linked to Christianity and that the democratic impulse has arisen in human history as a temporal manifestation of the inspiration of the Gospel.

> "The question does not deal here with Christianity as a religious creed (i.e., as *denomination*) and road to eternal life, but rather with Christianity as leaven in the social and political order of nations, and as bearer of the temporal hope of mankind ... it deals with Christianity as historical energy at work in the world. It is not in the heights of theology, it is in the depths of the secular conscience and secular existence that Christianity works in this fashion ... "[190]

We are indebted to Maritain, widely recognized as the preeminent Thomist of our times, for his incisive distinctions between person and individual and between denominational versus inspirational Christianity. They are critical to re-discovering an authentic anthropology and the genuine roots of democracy, as well as to the study of faith informing culture and the re-evangelizing of contemporary society. We will explore these distinctions shortly.

Chapter Eight: Religion and the Congress of the Confederation, 1774 -1789

"To the distinguished Character of Patriot, it should be our highest Glory to add the more distinguished Character of Christian." George Washington

The first national government of the United States was the Continental-Confederation Congress, which functioned from 1774 to 1789 when— by virtue of the Constitution— it was replaced by the newly created federal government. In a relatively brief period of time, with little official power and no permanent home, this remarkable group of men defeated the world's greatest military power, concluded America's most successful peace treaty, and put in place a remarkable plan for settling the American West.

"Equally remarkable," writes James Hutson, "was the energy Congress invested in encouraging the practice of religion throughout the new nation, energy that far exceeded the amount expended by any subsequent national government."[191]

An unusual number of deeply religious men held positions of national leadership in this Congress. There was Charles Thomson (1729-1804), "the soul of Congress and the source of its institutional continuity as its permanent secretary from 1774 to 1789."[192] Thomson retired from public life to translate the Scriptures from Greek to English. "The four-volume Bible that Thomson published in 1808 is admired by modern scholars for its accuracy and learning."

There was John Dickinson (1732-1808), "who, as the "Pennsylvania Farmer," was the colonies' premier political pamphleteer, and who, as a member of Congress in 1776, wrote the first draft of the *Articles of Confederation*."[193] Dickinson retired from public life to devote himself to religious scholarship, writing commentaries on the Gospel of Matthew.

There was Elias Boudinot (1740-1821), president of the Congress from 1782-1783, who tuned out "warm" debates on the floor to write his daughter long letters, praying that, through the blood of God's "too greatly despised Son," she should be "born again to the newness of Life." Boudinot resigned as director of the U.S. Mint in 1805 to write such religious tracts as *The Second Advent* (1815) and, the next year, became the first president of the American Bible Society.[194]

There was Henry Laurens (1724-1792), who was president of Congress, 1777-1778. Laurens was "strict and exemplary" in the performance of his religious duties, reading Scriptures diligently to his family, and "making all his children read them also."[195]

And there was John Jay (1745-1829), who succeeded Laurens as president of Congress, 1778-1779 and later served as first chief justice of the Supreme Court. Historian Richard Hildreth believed Jay was one of the "three granite pillars of America's political greatness;"

the three, which also included Washington and Hamilton, constituted "a trio not to be matched, in fact, not to be approached in our history."[196]

John Jay

John Jay, at the age of twenty-nine, was the youngest delegate to the 1774 Continental Congress. Noted for his sound judgment and wisdom, he was selected to prepare a draft of the United States' address asking Great Britain for redress of grievances. After helping complete the peace treaty that ended the war with England, Congress named him Secretary of Foreign Affairs.

Jay's son William described him as "a rare but interesting picture of the Christian patriot and statesman," always conscious of God's sovereign hand at work, both in his own life and in human affairs. His ancestors were French Huguenots (Calvinist Protestants), and Jay frequently referred to the "beneficent care of heaven" in sparing his family from religious persecution in France.[197]

Jay saw God's hand at work in the conflict between Britain and the United States, and his address in New York in support of the Declaration of Independence was filled with biblical references. He compared America with Israel and stated that God would not bless America's cause unless it was true to Him.

He insisted that America trust in God and not give itself over to selfish vice. He wrote: "Let a general reformation of manners take place — let universal charity, public spirit, and private virtue be inculcated, encouraged, and practiced. Unite in preparing for a vigorous defence of your country, as if all depended on your own exertions. And when you have done all things, then rely upon the good

Providence of Almighty God for success, in full confidence that without his blessings, all our efforts will inevitably fail."[198]

Jay concluded by saying that independence was part of God's plan for bringing the gospel to the Western world, and that God would give success to the cause of independence if Americans trusted God: "The holy gospels have yet to be preached to these western regions; and we have the highest reason to believe that the Almighty will not suffer slavery and the gospel go hand in hand. It cannot, it will not be."[199]

Extolled for "the firmness, even fervor, of his religious convictions," upon retiring from public life, Jay became president of the American Bible Society.[200]

As for mixing religion and politics, Jay distinguished the moral from the political, but in the interest of showing their relationship. He firmly believed the Christian faith should affect people's views of the political order, and exhorted pastors to speak out against that which is morally repugnant.

He once wrote, "Although the mere expedience of public measures may not be a proper subject for the pulpit, yet, in my opinion, it is the right and duty of our pastors to press the observance of all moral and religious duties, and to animadvert on every course of conduct which may be repugnant to them ..."[201]

Not surprisingly, with men like this forming the fledgling American government, Congress's first charge to its constituents was its resolution of June 12, 1775, setting a national day of "public humiliation, fasting and prayer" to be held five weeks later, on July 20.[202] The "Continental Fast," as it was called, did not disappoint those like John Adams, who predicted that "millions will be on their Knees at once before their great Creator, imploring His Forgiveness and Blessing, His Smiles on American Councils and Arms."[203]

On the appointed morning of the fast, Congress attended services and heard sermons at Reverend Jacob Duche's Anglican Church. (Duche was elected that body's first chaplain on July 9, 1776). Not wanting to patronize one denomination exclusively, in the after-noon it worshipped at Francis Alison's Presbyterian meeting. On July 4, 1779, Congress worshipped en mass at Philadelphia's "Roman Chapel," and at the "Dutch Lutheran Church" on October 24, 1781. After the Duche debacle —he defected to the British in 1777— Congress appointed joint chaplains of different denominations in an added effort to appear evenhanded in religious matters.[204]

The religiosity of the American people was such that for ten years, from the first fast-day proclamation of 1775 to the final thanksgiving proclamation of August 3, 1784, Congress repeatedly preached the political theology of a national covenant. Namely "the belief that the war with Britain was God's punishment for America's sins and that national confession and repentance would reconcile Him to the country and cause Him to bare His mighty arm and smite the British."[205]

One writer on the period of the American Revolution has stated that "the religious temper of America was one of the prime causes of the Revolution," which is borne out by the statement made by Edmund Burke before Parliament in his famous speech on "Conciliation."

Burke said:

> "In America, religious beliefs and practices were in advance of those of all other Protestants in the world. In America the people were accustomed to free and subtle

debate on all religious questions, and there was among them little regard for priests, councils or creeds. Their Church organizations were simple and democratic, as were those of the Congregationalists and Baptists, or republican as the Presbyterians, and they were accustomed to elect and dismiss their own religious leaders.

"In short, in America at the end of the colonial era there was a larger degree of religious liberty than was to be found among most of the people of the world, and possession of religious liberty naturally leads to a demand for political liberty."[206]

Religion and Society: Distinct, Not Separate

Samuel Williams was a Congregational minister, professor of mathematics and natural philosophy at Harvard, and a founder of the University of Vermont. A sermon by Williams in 1780 describes how the relationship between religion and society would work. Religion, Williams suggested, could be considered both a "private thing" and a "public concern." Religion was a "private thing" in the sense that the magistrate had no right whatsoever to determine its doctrines or modes of worship. It was a "public concern" in the sense that the state had an interest in supporting preachers, who, at the very least, were the "keepers of the morals of the people."[207]

"The religion of Jesus Christ," Williams wrote, "will be found to be well adapted to do the most essential service to Civil Society."[208] Williams's position on Christianity was fully supported by Congress, which took up the question of Bible supply in 1780, when it was moved that the states be requested "to procure one or more new and correct editions of the Old and New Testaments to be published."

The issue of Bible reading, then, was not one of separation, but of encouragement. Robert Aitken, a Philadelphia printer, was preparing a publication of the Old and New Testament at his own expense. On September 12, 1782, having asked its chaplains' opinions of his work, which they said was done "with great accuracy," Congress passed the following resolution: "The United States in Congress assembled, highly approve the pious and laudable undertaking of Mr. Aitken, as subservient to the interest of religion ... and being satisfied ... of his care and accuracy, recommend this edition of the Bible to the inhabitants of the United States."

Aitken's edition of the scriptures, published under congressional patronage, appeared shortly thereafter. It was the first English language Bible published on the North American continent.[209]

The Father of the Country—Washington

The most significant element of the Bill of Rights, which became law on December 15, 1791, was religion, as reflected in the First Amendment giving citizens freedom of religion, assembly, speech, press and petitioning. George Washington, who favored any law forbidding establishment of religion, saw the First Amendment as aimed at preventing the erection of a national Church of any denomination.

On the other hand, Washington, generally characterized as a deist rather than a Christian, could not be characterized as a "separationist," as his Farewell Address clearly demonstrates. And he would definitely not want to be called a non-Christian, and certainly not anti-Christian. "All his codes of morals, order, and propriety were rooted in Christianity, which he saw as the greatest civilizing force the world had ever known ... The notion that the First Amendment would be twisted into an instrument to prohibit the traditional practices of Christianity would have horrified him."[210]

Washington, in fact, had urged his fellow Virginians to appropriate public funds for teaching of religion. As a general in the revolutionary army, he required church attendance by his soldiers.[211] From his headquarters in Valley Forge, on May 2, 1778, he wrote the following: "While we are zealously performing the duties of good Citizens and Soldiers we certainly ought not to be inattentive to the higher duties of Religion. To the distinguished Character of Patriot, it should be our highest Glory to add the more distinguished Character of Christian."[212]

Historian Paul Johnson points out that Washington "served for many years as a vestryman of his local Anglican-style Church because he believed this to be a pointed gesture of solidarity with an institution he regarded as underpinning a civilized society. An America without religion as the strongest voluntary source of morality was, to him, an impossibility."[213]

As Washington observed in his famous Farewell Address, delivered to the American people on September 19, 1796, "whatever may be conceded to the influence of refined education on minds of peculiar structure, reason and experience both forbid us to expect that national morality can prevail in exclusion of religious principle."

The section on religion is highly revelatory of Washington's thoughts on religion:

> "Of all the dispositions and habits which lead to political prosperity, Religion and morality are indispensable supports. In vain would that man claim the tribute of Patriotism, who should labour to subvert these great

Pillars of human happiness, these firmest props of the duties of Men and citizens. The mere Politician, equally with the pious man ought to respect and to cherish them. A volume could not trace all their connections with private and public felicity. Let it simply be asked where is the security for property, for reputation, for life, if the sense of religious obligation deserts the oaths, which are the instruments of investigation in Courts of Justice?

"And let us with caution indulge the supposition, *that morality can be maintained without religion.* Whatever may be conceded to the influence of refined education on minds of peculiar structure, reason and experience both forbid us to expect that National morality can prevail in exclusion of religious principle. 'Tis substantially true, that virtue or morality is a necessary spring of popular government. The rule indeed extends with more and less force to every species of free Government." [214]

As for Washington's notion of tolerance extending beyond Christianity, there is the following anecdote. On August 15, 1790, the President and Secretary of State Thomas Jefferson left New York City, the temporary capital of the United States, for a brief tour of Rhode Island.

At Newport, Washington received an address of congratulations from the congregation of the Touro Synagogue, the oldest synagogue building in North America, built in 1763. His famous answer, a copy of which can be found in the Library of Congress, assured his fellow citizens "of the Stock of Abraham" that the new American republic would give "to bigotry no sanction, to persecution no assistance."[215]

The influence and relationship of Judaism to democracy is a significant and scholarly topic, beyond the province of this book. Suffice it to note an article in the *Wall Street Journal,* entitled "The Whispers of Democracy in Ancient Judaism." Its author, Eric Rosenberg, points to the significance of the call to monotheism, virtuous conduct and personal responsibility for the Jewish people nearly four millennia ago.

He notes University of Chicago scholar William E. Irwin lecturing in the 1940s that it was the ancient Jewish prophets and their advocacy of freedom that would find an early expression in the *Magna Carta* and, later, in the American Bill of Rights.[216]

Democracy and Virtue

The Founders shared the thought of their British contemporary Edmund Burke: "We know and what is better, we inwardly feel, that religion is the basis of civil society, and the source of all good and of all comfort."[217]

At the same time the "religiosity" of the Founders was not restricted to pietism and prayer. As students of history and of the classics they were keenly aware of the dangers of a normless, amoral culture. They firmly believed that an openness to the transcendent—a higher order of self-evident truths —helped facilitate a virtuous citizenry that could follow a moral code.

James Madison rhetorically inquired: "Is there no virtue among us? If there be not, we are in a wretched situation ... To suppose that any form of government will secure liberty or happiness without any virtue in the people is a chimerical idea."[218]

Madison knew that the political order must comport with natural law, and called government "the greatest of all reflections on human nature."[219]

Russell Kirk put it this way: "Out of faith arises order; and once order prevails, freedom becomes possible. When the faith that nurtured the order fades away, the order disintegrates; and freedom no more can survive the disappearance of order than the branch of a tree can outlast the fall of the trunk."[220]

The fact is that the new American order established by the Founders was constituted of Judeo-Christian religious traditions as well as classical philosophical insights. This is why the Founders could presume a certain degree of virtue in the people, and how they could propose a system of government that was, as John Adams said, "made only for moral and religious people."[221]

Chapter Nine: The Second Great Awakening

The enduring religiosity of the American people is reflected in the Second Great Awakening, essentially a Protestant revival movement during the early nineteenth century in the United States. Beginning in around 1790, the notion of restoring more "primitive" forms of Christianity in America grew in popularity. It represented the desire to restore a purer form of Christianity, without an elaborate hierarchy, and contributed to the development of many groups during this time, including the Mormons, the Baptists and the Shakers.

The Second Awakening has been described as a reaction against skepticism, deism and rational Christianity. The decade and a half following the close of the American Revolution was one of spiritual deadness among all the American Churches. A historian of the Episcopalians characterized the period from the close of the war to 1812 as one of "suspended animation."[222]

This was not true of the Episcopalians alone. It was indeed, "the period of the lowest ebb-tide of vitality in the history of American Christianity."[223]

Lyman Beecher (1775-1836), as a student at Yale College in 1795, describes in his interesting *Reminiscences* the religious condition in the college at that time: "The College was in the most ungodly state. The college Church was almost extinct. Most of the students were skeptical, and rowdies were plenty. Wine and liquors were kept in many rooms, intemperance, profanity, gambling, and licentiousness were common." Beecher recalls how Tom Paine was in great vogue among the young men, "and boys came to college boasting of their infidelity and addressing one another as Voltaire, Rousseau, d'Alembert, etc."[224]

Deistic influence, described by the orthodox as "the spirit of half belief or unbelief" and coming from both England and France, was particularly strong at this time. Numerous Jocabin clubs and societies of the Illuminati arose in the country, "devoting their energies to the ridicule of Christianity and to bringing in the *Age of Reason*."[225]

Furthermore, "So low were the fortunes of the Protestant Episcopal Church at this period that even some of the bishops looked for it to die out with the old colonial families. So hopeless did Bishop Samuel Provoost of New York consider the religious situation that he ceased functioning, while Bishop James Madison of Virginia, we are told, shared the conviction of Chief Justice Marshall, himself a devout Churchman, that the Church "was too far gone ever to be revived."[226]

The resolute Lyman Beecher did not share this conviction. Beecher was a New Haven Presbyterian who "went west" and eventually became president of the Lane Theological Seminary. He was father of thirteen children, most notably daughter Harriet Beecher Stowe, author of *Uncle Tom's Cabin*. Beecher believed a revivalist spirit was essential to the creation of the rapidly expanding American nation.[227] He discovered that Churches cut loose from the dependence on state support found a renewed vigor and forcefulness.

Led by men such as Beecher, as well as the pioneer Baptist John Taylor, who visited Kentucky for the first time in 1779 and worked in the new West, and the outstanding leader at the beginning of the revival in the West, Presbyterian minister James McGready, the Second Awakening gained momentum by 1800. After 1820, membership rose rapidly among Baptist and Methodist congregations.

Relying on their own resources and on God, the churches and synagogues of America began moving forward with swift and astonishing speed, not only to check the spread of infidelity but also to meet the challenges of a rapidly moving frontier and expanding population.[228]

Voluntarism

"Voluntarism," that is, action unaided by the state and undirected by any supreme ecclesiastical authority, came to be the distinguishing feature of religion in America, and at no time more conspicuously so than in the early decades of the nineteenth century.[229]

Robert Baird (1798-1863), one of the first historians of America's religious experiment, explained to Europeans that what was happening in the United States was different from anything they had known. The difference lay chiefly in "the voluntary" principle. This principle, Baird noted, represented an energy and self-reliance that extended itself "in every direction with an all-powerful influence." By means of voluntary religious associations, men and women became instruments of this new force "wherever the Gospel is to be preached, wherever vice is to be attacked, wherever suffering humanity is to be relieved."[230]

Not without relevance to our own times, Paul Johnson observes that this period's commitment to a free market, in land and everything else, "was necessarily driven by a strong current of materialist individuals. Beecher felt only religious belief and practice, hot and strong, could supply the spiritual leavening and community spirit; could, in effect, civilize this thrusting people."[231]

Religion, politics and culture all went together, he argued, "and it is plain that the religious and political destiny of the nation is to be decided in the West." This Awakening was essentially a frontier affair, and while Episcopalians and other older Churches discounted the camp meeting approach, the uninhibited Methodists profited a great deal from revivalism, or what is now called fundamentalism. They kept up its passionate intensity and continued drumming it into their regular, settled congregations, such that by 1844 Methodists were the largest denomination in the United States.[232]

Bishop Francis Asbury, one of the leading Methodist advocates of the camp meeting, estimated that, in 1811, between three and four million Americans were attending such events each summer; that was about a third of the population of the entire country.

As for the Baptists, they radiated out from Rhode Island and its great theological seminary, later Brown University (1764). They split from time to time, as did most Calvinist sects, generating such factions as Separatist and Hard-Shell Baptists. But they were enormously successful in the South and West, and by 1850 had penetrated every existing state and had a major theological college in almost all of them.[233]

Some of the South's greatest institutions of higher education have their origins in the Second Great Awakening. The leading theologian of the Awakening, Charles Grandison Finney (1792-1875), founded Oberlin College in Ohio in 1844. Finney led revivals not only in the growing towns of westward migration but also and perhaps with greater effectiveness, in the major cities of the East.

Finney believed in the "cause and effect" approach to religion, namely that "just as we will reap a natural crop if we have done our work properly, so we will reap a supernatural crop of converts only if we have done our work properly. One is as scientifically and philosophically certain as the other: proper means lead to worthy ends."[234]

Finney was deeply convinced that the tepidity of the Churches was causing souls to be lost; "more than five thousand million have gone down to hell, while the Church has been dreaming, and waiting for God to save them without the use of means. Now is the time, and America the place, to show the willingness and enthusiasm of Christians to gather as many lost sheep as possible into the Churchly fold."[235]

Revivals stressed an individual response to Christian proclamations, and, in the process, gave impetus to renewed and enlarged Church membership. The Second Awakening, for example, gave impulse to Unitarians, who had come to America in the 1770s and opened King's College Chapel in Boston. The American Unitarian Association was formed in 1825 and quickly spread all over America, particularly attracting intellectuals and scientists with its low-key ritual and rationalist approach to theology.

While religious fervor died down in America after 1840, occasional revivals continued into the 1840s and 1850s, and the spiritual influence of the Second Awakening continued in the form of more secular movements. Amid shifts in theology and Church organization, American Christianity began progressive movements to reform society during this period. Commonly known as antebellum reform, this phenomenon extended to reforms in temperance, abolitionism, women's rights and a variety of other questions facing society.

The role of women in the Second Awakening was significant; they made up the majority of converts and participants during the Awakening and played a crucial role in its development and focus. Despite a lack of formal leadership roles, through family structure and their maternal role, women became very important in the conversion and religious upbringing of their children.

During the period of the revivals, religion was often passed on to children through the teaching and influence of mothers, who were seen as the moral and spiritual foundation of the family. Women's prayer was seen by leaders such as Charles Finney as crucial to preparing a community for revival, and improving their efficacy.[236]

The Second Great Awakening expressed Arminian theology, by which every person could be saved through revivals, repentance and conversion. Its main tenets were that election (and condemnation on the day of judgment) was conditioned by the rational faith or non-faith of man; the Atonement, while qualitatively adequate for all men, is efficacious only for the man of faith; unaided by the Holy Spirit, no person is able to respond to God's will; grace is resistible; and believers are able to resist sin but are not beyond the possibility of falling from grace.

The crux of Remonstrant Arminianism lay in the assertion that human dignity requires an unimpaired freedom of the will. Many Christian denominations have been influenced by Arminian views, notably the Baptists in the sixteenth century, the Methodists, the Congregationalists of the early New England colonies in the seventeenth and eighteenth centuries, and the Universalists and Unitarians in the eighteenth and nineteenth centuries.

Denominations such as the Anabaptists (beginning in 1525), Waldensians (pre-Reformation), and other groups prior to the Reformation have also held this view of the free will of man. Separation of Church and state seemed not a factor in the Second Awakening, at least at the practical level.

The Second Great Awakening stimulated the establishment of many reform movements designed to remedy the evils of society before the anticipated Second Coming of Jesus Christ.[237]

It enrolled millions of new members in existing evangelical denominations and led to the formation of new denominations. Many converts believed that the Awakening heralded a new millennial age. There was also a new political enthusiasm arising in America that seemed to echo the religious enthusiasm. More active participation in politics by more segments of the population brought religious and moral issues into the political sphere.

Historians stress the understanding, common among participants, of reform being part of God's plan. Local churches began to see their role in society as that of purifying the world through individuals to whom they would bring salvation, along with changes in the law and creation of new institutions. Transforming the world began to apply to mainstream political action through activism in antislavery and temperance movements, by virtue of implementing religious beliefs into national politics. Protestant religions played an even more important role in the American political scene due to the Second Great Awakening.

Chapter Ten: Lincoln and our Founders

"If we could first know where we are, and whither we are tending, we could better judge what to do, and how to do it." Abraham Lincoln

Abraham Lincoln, perhaps best among all of our presidents, understood the linkage between religion, morals and an enduring republic. Whatever his Church-going habits, Lincoln often declared himself a Christian. He read and quoted the Bible regularly and for periods of his life read it daily. It was, in fact, his first school-book. And he was convinced that Christian belief was not an obstacle but an abettor of freedom and of democracy.

Which is why —facing the horror of war— his inaugural words sound almost like a prayer, seeking God's help and the wisdom of our Founders to guide him through the terrible days ahead. Days that would eventually extend that freedom, grounded on Lincoln's indomitable faith in Providence, to all the peoples of this land and maintain the unity of a remarkable nation.

Also far better than most, Lincoln knew his history. And perhaps, in that inaugural, Lincoln was thinking of some of his great predecessors. Men such as Thomas Jefferson, author of the Declaration of Independence, who, while advocating separation of Church and state, had no problem with the underlying bond of democracy and religion.

Jefferson once wrote, "Can the liberties of a nation be thought secure when we have removed their only firm basis, a conviction in the minds of the people that these liberties are of the gift of God? That they are not to be violated but with his wrath."[238] A summation of these words is now permanently engraved on the walls of the Jefferson Memorial in Washington D.C.

On the Northwest interior wall of his memorial is an excerpt from Jefferson's "A Bill for Establishing Religious Freedom, 1777." It reads, in part, "Almighty God hath created the mind free—All attempts to influence it by temporal punishments or burthens—are a departure from the plan of the Holy Author of our religion—all men shall be free to profess and by argument to maintain, their opinions in matters of religion."

Or perhaps Lincoln was thinking of "the Father of the Constitution," a stalwart defender of religious liberties and former president, James Madison. Madison was raised in a strong Episcopalian home; both parents were active in the Church, and he attended the College of New Jersey (now Princeton), then a very orthodox, conservative Christian school. Of the Constitution Madison wrote, "The future and success of America is not in this Constitution but in the laws of God upon which this Constitution is founded."[239]

This is how Madison put it in his *Memorial and Remonstrance,* one of the key texts in shaping the American constitutional tradition of religious freedom:

"It is the duty of every man to render to the Creator such homage and such as only as he believes to be acceptable to him. This duty is precedent both in order of time and in degree of obligation, to the claims of Civil Society. Before any man can be considered as a member of Civil Society, he must be considered as a subject of the Governor of the Universe. And if a member of Civil Society, who enters into any subordinate Association, must always do it with a reservation of his duty to the General Assembly; much more must every man who becomes a member of any particular Civil Society do it with a saving of his allegiance to the Universal Sovereign."[240]

As for Christianity, Madison believed the Christian faith strong enough doctrinally, theologically, morally, and intellectually that it did not need the support of civil government. Furthermore, "it was because Madison exalted religion that he favored religious liberty. Since he revered the Christian religion above all others, he wanted it to flourish in its purity, free from the corruption that inevitably came from state support."[241]

Madison called conscience man's "most sacred of all property; other property depending in part on positive law, the exercise of that being a natural and unalienable right. To guard a man's house as his castle, to pay public and enforce private debts with the most exact faith, can give no title to invade a man's conscience, which is more sacred than his castle, or to withhold from it that debt of protection for which the public faith is pledged by the very nature and original conditions of the social pact."[242]

John Adams

John Adams, the second president of the United States, a founding father, and a self-confessed "Church-going animal," held views similar to Jefferson. Adams felt acutely the responsibility of living up to his family heritage: the founding generation of Puritans who believed "they lived in the Bible. England under the Stuarts was Egypt; they were Israel, fleeing ... to establish a refuge for godliness, a city upon a hill."[243]

Adams, a Unitarian whose wife, Abigail, was the daughter of a Congregational minister, was a serious Christian who credited religion with the success of his ancestors' migration to the new world in the 1630s. He vigorously denounced Thomas Paine's criticisms of Christianity, saying, "The Christian religion is, above all the religions that ever prevailed or existed in ancient or modern times, the religion of wisdom, virtue, equity and humanity, let the Blackguard Paine say what he will."[244]

Adams contended, in fact, that: "Religion and virtue are the only foundations, not only of republicanism and of all free governments, but of social felicity under all governments and in all combinations of human society."[245]

He once wrote: "The general principles on which the Fathers achieved independence ... were the general principles of Christianity ... Now I avow that I then believed (and now believe) that those general principles of Christianity are as eternal and immutable as the existence and attributes of God. In favor of these general principles in philosophy, religion, and government I could fill sheets of quotations from ... philosophers including Locke—not to mention thousands of divines and philosophers of inferior fame."[246]

Fisher Ames, who drafted the wording for the First Amendment, also wrote that the Bible—which he believed was the Word of God and a true source of wisdom—should remain the principal text book of America's classroom. "Its morals are pure, its examples are captivating and noble."[247]

John Quincy Adams

John Quincy Adams was John Adams's son and our sixth president (1825-1829). He is also one of America's greatest congressmen and diplomats, not only of the colonial era but in American history. Adams was also recognized as a fierce and consistent foe of slavery. After one of his reelections to Congress, for example, he said that he must "bring about a day prophesied when slavery and war shall be banished from the face of the earth."[248]

He wrote: "It is among the evils of slavery that it taints the very sources of moral principle. It establishes false estimates of virtue and vice: for what can be more false and heartless than this doctrine which makes the first and holiest rights of humanity to depend upon the color of the skin?" [249]

Adams, a remarkably devout man, came a generation after the Founders and shared in their religious conviction. For years he made it a practice to read through the Bible, once each year. He wrote: "From the Declaration of Independence, the American people were bound by the laws of God and the laws of the Gospel of Jesus Christ, which they all acknowledge as the roots of their conduct. We all came together to obey the word of God."[250]

Adams clearly saw, among all of its precepts, the primacy of charity in the Christian religion. He wrote:

> "The fundamental doctrine of the Christian religion is the extirpation of hatred from the human heart. It forbids the

exercise of it, even towards enemies. There is no denomination of Christians which denies or misunderstands this doctrine. All understand it alike — all acknowledge its obligations; and however imperfectly, in the purposes of Divine Providence, its efficacy has been shown in the practice of Christians, it has not been wholly inoperative upon them.

"Its effect has been upon the manners of nations. It has mitigated the horrors of war — it has softened the features of slavery — it has humanized the intercourse of social life. The unqualified acknowledgements of a duty does not, indeed, suffice to insure its performance.

"Hatred is yet a passion, but too powerful upon the hearts of Christians, yet they cannot indulge it, except by the sacrifice of their principles, and the conscious violation of their duties. No state paper from a Christian hand, could, without trampling the precepts of its Lord and Master, have commenced by an open proclamation of hatred in any portion of the human race."[251]

Adams was known as a great orator. When he feared that Christian influence was waning in New England, he prepared a lecture on truth that he delivered in many places. The premise was: "A man to be a Christian must believe in God, in the Bible, in the Divinity of the Savior's mission, and in a future state of rewards and punishments."[252]

Religion of the Founders

From a purely statistical perspective it's fair to say that all of the men who might be considered founding fathers of America —this would include the fifty-six signers of the Declaration of Independence, the forty-eight signers of the Articles of Confederation, and all fifty-five delegates who participated in the Constitutional Convention of 1787 —were Christian. The largest denominational affiliations for these men were Episcopalian/Anglican (54.7 percent), Presbyterian (18.6 percent), and Congregationalist (16.8 percent). [253]

The signers of the Declaration of Independence were a profoundly intelligent, religious and ethically-minded group. The Declaration signers were members of religious denominations at a rate significantly higher than average for the American Colonies in the late 1700s. Four of the signers were current or former full-time preachers, and many more were the sons of clergymen.

These signers were admired both by secularists, who appreciated the non-denominational nature of the Declaration, and by traditional religionists, who appreciated the Declaration's recognition of God as the source of rights enumerated by the documents. Prolific American historian B.J. Lossing's seminal collection of biographies of the signers of the Declaration of Independence echoed widely held sentiments, then and now, that there was a divine intent or inspiration behind the Declaration.

Lossing matter-of-factly identified the signers as "instruments of Providence" who have "gone to receive their reward in the Spirit Land.[254]

As for Abraham Lincoln and the Declaration, it should be said that Lincoln made it the centerpiece of his rhetoric (as in the Gettysburg Address of 1863), as well as his policies. Lincoln considered it to be the foundation of his political philosophy, and argued that the Declaration is a statement of principles through which the U.S.

Constitution should be interpreted. Since then, it has become a major statement on human rights, particularly its second sentence:

We hold these truths to be self-evident, that all men are created equal, that they are endowed by their Creator with certain unalienable Rights, that among these are Life, Liberty and the pursuit of Happiness.

This has been called "one of the best-known sentences in the English language," containing "the most potent and consequential words in American history."[255] The passage came to represent a moral standard to which the United States should strive. The American Declaration of Independence, of course, has inspired work for the rights of marginalized people throughout the world, as well as numerous national declarations of independence.

Chapter Eleven: More Recent Times

"In love, which is the very essence of the message of the Prince of Peace, the world would find a solution for all its ills." Harry S. Truman

The current Health and Human Services debate shows how easy it is to forget where the hard-won values proper to democracy originate. A relevant reminder is a message by Franklin Roosevelt on January 4, 1939, at the beginning of World War II.

Fascism, Nazism, and, ultimately, Communism were presenting the greatest threats to democratic ideals in the twentieth century—indeed in history. Walter Lippmann, referring to Roosevelt's speech, said it contained "the outline of that reconstruction of their moral philosophies which the democracies must undertake if they are to survive."[256]

In his address, Roosevelt stressed that democracy, respect for the human person, for liberty and for international good faith, find their soundest foundation in religion and furnish religion with its best guarantee. He later affirmed, in a letter of January 17, 1942 (to American bishops no less!) that "we (the United Nations) should seek ... the establishment of an international order in which the spirit of Christ shall rule the hearts of men and of nations."[257]

Several months later, in an important speech by Henry A. Wallace, the vice president of the United States declared that, "The idea of freedom — is derived from the Bible with its extraordinary emphasis on the dignity of the individual. Democracy is the only true political expression of Christianity."[258]

That same year, a charter was adopted by the New Education Fellowship Conference, meeting in London. Its six points included the following provisions: "The right of every child to proper food, clothing and shelter must henceforth be assured by the nation as its responsibility; medical treatment must be available for all; all must have equal opportunities to full-time schooling; *and there must be universal religious training.*"[259](emphasis added).

President Truman

At the end of World War II, during the lighting of the Christmas tree on White House grounds, President Harry S. Truman spoke these moving words:

> "This is the Christmas that a war-weary world has prayed for through long and awful years. With peace come joy and gladness. The gloom of the war years fades as once more we light the National Community Christmas Tree. We meet in the spirit of the first Christmas, when the midnight choir sang the hymn of joy: 'Glory to God in the highest, and on earth peace, good will toward men.'

"Let us not forget that the coming of the Saviour brought a time of long peace to the Roman World. It is, therefore, fitting for us to remember that the spirit of Christmas is the spirit of peace, of love, of charity to all men. From the manger of Bethlehem came a new appeal to the minds and hearts of men: 'A new commandment I give unto you, that you love one another.'

"In love, which is the very essence of the message of the Prince of Peace, the world would find a solution for all its ills. I do not believe there is one problem in this country or in the world today, which could not be settled if approached through the teaching of the Sermon on the Mount." [260]

Perhaps it's not surprising, in reading these words, to learn that in his youth Truman had read the family Bible through three times, as well as all the books in the Independence, Missouri, public library, including the encyclopedias.[261] Or that he used two Bibles during his swearing-in on January 20, 1949; a personal one he had used for the first oath, and a Gutenberg Bible donated by the citizens of his home-town. After the oath, like Andrew Jackson before him, Truman quickly bent and kissed the Bible.[262]

Truman found in the Bible the moral core of the American system of government. In March 1952, he told the convention of the Columbia Scholastic Press Association that:

"The fundamental basis of this Nation's ideals was given to Moses on Mount Sinai. The fundamental basis of the Bill of Rights of our Constitution comes from the teachings which we get from Exodus, St. Matthew, Isaiah, and St. Paul. The Sermon on the Mount gives us a way of life, and maybe someday men will understand it as the real way of life. The basis of all great moral codes is 'Do unto others as you would have others do unto you.' Treat others as you would like to be treated."[263]

Truman added that, while some may think that such a philosophy as that has no place in politics and government, it is the only philosophy on which to base a lasting government. Governments built on that philosophy are built on a rock and will not fail.

On March 5, 1946, nine months after Sir Winston Churchill failed to be reelected as Britain's Prime Minister, President Truman accompanied him by train to the small Missouri town of Fulton to make his now-famous "Iron Curtain" speech. It was perhaps Churchill's most famous post-war speech, wherein he warned of the need to "never cease to proclaim in fearless tones the great principles of freedom and the rights of man — which find their most famous expression in the American Declaration of Independence."

In grave tones, Churchill signaled the threat of ideological atheism to democracy and to Europe's future. He exhorted "a new unity in Europe" to deal with the threat of future wars, and especially with Communist expansion throughout Europe, "from Stettin in the Baltic to Trieste in the Adriatic," which "constitute a growing challenge and peril to Christian civilization."[264]

Jacques Maritain, a prominent drafter of the United Nations Charter on the *Universal Declaration of Human Rights* in 1948 (whose purpose, in no small part, was to extend the basic values of democracy globally after the war, and which has been essentially ratified by all the world's countries, including Muslim), took this relationship between democracy and Christianity a step further.

Article 18 of the *Universal Declaration of Human Rights* states that, "Everyone has the right to freedom of thought, conscience and religion; this right includes freedom to change his religion or belief, and freedom, either alone or in community with others and in public or private, to manifest his religion or belief in teaching, practice, worship and observance."

The proclamation was ratified during the General Assembly on December 10, 1948, by a vote of forty-eight in favor, zero against, with eight abstentions.

Maritain wrote in 1943, at the height of World War II, "not only does the democratic state of mind stem from the inspiration of the Gospel, but it cannot exist without it." He quoted his mentor Henri Bergson: "Democracy is evangelical in essence and ... its motive power is love."[265] And he was keenly aware of the unique history and beneficence of the American form of government.

For example, in his book *Man and the State,* Maritain wrote, "The Constitution of this country is deep-rooted in the age-old heritage of Christian civilization. This Constitution can be described as an outstanding lay Christian document tinged with the philosophy of the day. The spirit and inspiration of this great political Christian document is basically repugnant to the idea of making human society stand aloof from God and from any religious faith."[266]

As the great historian of Christian culture Christopher Dawson — often called the historian of change — wrote, "In the last resort every civilization is built on a religious foundation: it is the expression in social institutions and cultural activity of a faith or vision of reality which gives the civilization its spiritual unity. Thus the great world cultures correspond with the great world religions and when a religion dies the civilization that it inspired gradually decays."[267]

This reinforces Maritain's point—and that of the Founders—namely that without the spiritual dynamism and rectitude of a living Christianity, political judgment is vulnerable to the forces of power, selfishness and ignorance that can dominate even a free society. And Maritain is careful to point out that "the question does not deal here with Christianity as a religious creed and road to eternal life but rather with Christianity as leaven in the social and political life of nations as bearers of the temporal hope of mankind ... as historical energy at work in the world".[268]

Maritain's challenges extend, however, not just to government but to those governed as well. With remarkable prescience (he was writing in the late 1930s), Maritain indicts the lack of participation of Catholics in social and political matters. He writes, "... Catholics too long considered that it was enough for them in-so-far as social matters were concerned, to rest upon the structures of existing civilization (precisely because they were of Christian origin), without undertaking in this order any personal action of a properly social nature. We are now paying for this optimism, which —especially after the victory of the liberal and capitalist economy — too often led to egoism and sins of omission."[269]

Chapter Twelve: The Apostasy of Europe— Can it Happen Here?

"All the countries of Europe are imbued with Christian civilization. This is the soul of Europe, it must be reborn." Robert Schuman

I t took fully 1,500 years of Christian influence, as Hegel noted, for the freedom of the person to begin to flourish. The seedbed and greatest manifestation of this flourishing was, of course, in Europe.

One of the many paradoxes of modern Europe's 'forgetfulness' of its profound evangelical roots—as evidenced by its massively destructive world wars in the twentieth century, and more recently by its refusal to include any reference to Christianity or an *invocatio Dei* in its European Constitution—is that its founding fathers: Konrad Adenauer of Germany, Alcide De Gasperi from Italy, and Robert Schuman of France, were men of remarkable Christian conviction.

All in fact were deeply religious Catholics—beatification processes are underway for all three men—and all suffered greatly, both for their countries under Nazism and Fascism, and for their personal convictions.[270]

The other "father" of the European Union, Jean Monnet (1888-1979), was also a devout Roman Catholic. Monnet, often regarded as the chief architect of European unity, was a French political economist and diplomat. He was sent to the United States in August, 1940 by the British government to negotiate the purchase of war supplies. He soon became an advisor to President Franklin D. Roosevelt and —convinced that America could serve as "the great arsenal of democracy" —persuaded the president to launch a massive arms production program to supply the Allies with military material.

After the war, British economist John Maynard Keynes said that Monnet's coordinating efforts probably shortened World War II by a full year. His international reputation was such that in December 1963 Monnet was presented with the Presidential Medal of Freedom, with special distinction, by President Lyndon Johnson.[271]

As for De Gasperi, when he addressed the first European Parliament in 1949 in the Palace of Europe in Strasbourg, it was generally acclaimed that he had provided the basic idea on which post-war peace could be built. Above all, he emphasized the absolute neces-sity of a joint ideal of unity and a substitute for the dangerous ideal of nationalism, which had caused so much evil. In 1952 De Gasperi received the Charles the Great Prize, conferred on "the most emi-nent European," for his work of championing the cause of interna-tional understanding.[272]

The Schuman Declaration—clearly based on natural law— is recog-nized as the founding document of the European Union; the day of its declaration, May 9, 1950, was five years and one day after Victory in Europe Day, when Germany surrendered. In his book *For Europe*, Robert Schuman, a modest, celibate biblical scholar who served twice as Prime Minster of France, describes its underlying motif: "Democracy owes its existence to Christianity— all the countries of Europe are imbued with Christian civilization. This is the soul of Europe, it must be reborn."[273]

The point of mentioning these visionary European Founders is that none of them were Pollyannish ideologues, intellectualists or abstractionists, much less religious romantics. They were tough, practical realists with vast political experience, which the enormous challenges of a devastated post-war Europe demanded. They clearly realized Europe needed resurgent economies, democratic values and free enterprise to build a truly sustainable future. But they also recognized the need for restoration of what we might call Europe's "fourth dimension," grounded on its prodigious religious past.

Each of these men had struggled mightily with secular rulers, most notably Mussolini and Hitler, who claimed authority, not only over men as citizens but over their consciences and their religious allegiance. They believed Europe needed a new vision and a renewed faith, at a vibrant cultural level, in what it had been and what it could become. Radical secularism had severely betrayed Europe in the twentieth century. Only a lived Christianity, they believed, could be the spirit and foundation for an authentically European Union going forward.[274]

An interesting aside is that the European Union's flag — a circle of twelve yellow stars on a blue background — carries a benign Christian message. Arsène Heitz, a French Catholic who designed the flag in 1955, drew inspiration from Christian iconography of the

Virgin Mary wearing a crown with twelve stars. The same twelve stars appear on all euro coins.

As for a lived Christianity, one of the great Europeans of our times, Pope John Paul II, offered this prescription for responding to the challenges of New Europe:

> "European identity does not make sense without Christianity. It is precisely in it (Christianity) that we find those shared roots from which the continent's civilization has grown: its culture, dynamism, activity and its ability to spread and build up other continents as well; all, in a word, that makes up its glory.[275]

> "If Europe acts once more in the area of spiritual life, with a proper knowledge and respect for God, on which all rights and justice are based; if Europe again opens its doors to Christ and is not afraid to open state boundaries, financial political systems, the vast fields of culture, civilization and development to His saving power, her future will not be ruled by uncertainty and fear; she will see a new era burgeon in her life and spirit, enhancing and shaping the whole world."[276]

As for intellectual amnesia spreading to other shores, it is also interesting to note that literature in English on Schuman, declared by the European Parliamentary Assembly as "Father of Europe," is virtually non-existent. As for rebirth of the Christian religion in Europe, it seems doubly ironic, given the undeniable historical reality and the transparent dispositions of the EU Founders, that there is such deafening silence regarding religion and Christianity in the European Constitution.

This constitution has been ratified by all EU members— now 28 countries with the accession of Croatia on 1 July 2013— many of them with once predominately Christian populations. [277]

At the same time the European Parliament has been calling for same-sex marriages to be recognized across the EU.[278] The Parliament rejected Rocco Buttiglione, a Roman Catholic, as Justice Commissioner in 2004, while at the same time approving Peter Mandelson, who is gay, as Trade Commissioner.

Cardinal Ratzinger, examining the objections to referencing Christianity in the preamble to the European Charter, had this to say:

> "Who would be offended by this? Whose identity is threatened thereby? The Muslims, who so often tend to be mentioned in this context, feel threatened, not by the foundations of our Christian morality, but by the cynicism of a secularized culture that denies its own foundations.

> "Nor are our Jewish fellow citizens offended by the reference to the Christian roots of Europe, since these roots go back to Mount Sinai and bear the imprint of the voice that rang out on the mountain of God. We are united with the Jews in those great basic orientations given to man by the Ten Commandments.

> "The same applies to the reference to God: it is not the mention of God that offends those who belong to other religions; rather it is the attempt to construct the human community in a manner that absolutely excludes God." [279]

As Michael Pakaluk has pointed out, the lesson many onlookers drew from all this is that believing the teachings of the Catholic

Church disqualifies one to serve in the government of Europe, which was midwifed by Catholics, no less. "The supposedly neutral and inclusive secularism which was to be enshrined in the European Constitution, it seemed, excluded all Catholics, all Orthodox Jews, many Protestants and most Muslims."[280]

It is indeed curious where the lines of toleration are drawn these days. Buttiglione's response to all this is a poignant description of the state of European affairs: "The new soft totalitarianism that is advancing on the left wants to have a state religion. It is an atheist, nihilistic religion — but it is a religion that is obligatory for all," he complained. Or, as Solzhenitsyn put it: "Europe is undergoing a civilizational crisis precipitated by a loss of higher intuition that comes from God."[281]

Acknowledging at least an awareness of that loss, on November 5, 2012, before a synod of Germany's Lutheran Church (Evangelische Kirche Deutschlands or EKD), German Chancellor Angela Merkel's address in Timmendorfer Strand in the German province of Schleswig-Holstein included the passing comment that "Christianity is the most persecuted religion in the world."[282]

Angela Merkel is the daughter of a Lutheran minister. Despite being publicly reserved about her religious beliefs, Merkel once referred to Germany as adhering to the larger, overall Christian ethic. "We feel bound to the Christian image of humanity —that is what defines us. Those who do not accept this are in the wrong place here."[283] The German federal government had thus made the protection of religious freedom, including that of Christians, into a goal of German foreign policy.

The secularization of Europe dramatizes that abandoning historically authentic religious values, whatever liberation and euphoria it may seem to provide, in the long run is intellectually destabilizing and culturally debilitating. It leads, among other ailments, to poverty of spirit, to a loss of identity and moral energy, to a lack of unity, and to ethical deficit. In Christopher Dawson's terms, it points to a "spiritual no-man's land."

It also leads to demographic suicide; no European birth rates are presently at replacement levels. Western European nations today report some of the lowest birth rates ever, causing Philip Jenkins to comment that "in demographic terms, modern Europe seems to have embarked on a self-destructive social experiment unprecedented in human history; what some have called slow-motion autogenocide."[284]

All of which encourages a spiritual impotence to deal with the rising tides of immigration, the emergence of significant Islamic populations, and a mixed strategy of appeasement and toughness toward radicalized Islam, as experiences in France give witness. And it leads to a future that George Weigel calls "procedural democracy," where moral truth has no longer any role in governance.[285]

As for some hard data on the ethical deficit aspect, the proportion of babies born to unmarried women is about 66 percent in Iceland, 55 percent in Sweden, 50 percent in France and 44 percent in the United Kingdom.[286] The United States appears anxious to catch up: roughly 40 percent of babies now born in the U.S. are to unmarried mothers, a sharp rise in recent years.

However much we wish to turn our heads, the social and cultural ramifications of all this are demonstrable. Children born to unmarried mothers are more likely to grow up in a single-parent household, experience instability in living arrangements, live in poverty, and have socio-emotional problems.

As these children reach adolescence, they are more likely to have low educational attainment, engage in sex at younger ages, and have a premarital birth. As young adults, children born outside of marriage are more likely to be idle (neither in school nor employed), have lower occupational status and income, and have more troubled marriages and divorces than those born to married parents.

Women who give birth outside of marriage tend to be more disadvantaged than their married counterparts, both before and after having a non-marital birth. Unmarried mothers generally have lower incomes, lower education levels, and greater dependence on welfare assistance than do married mothers. Women who have a non-marital birth also tend to fare worse than single women; for example, they have reduced marriage prospects compared to single women without children.[287]

Are We There Yet?

And the question is then, for us Americans: Have we also given up on our religious identity? Are we also losing our moral footing, abandoning our historic institutions to bogus ideology, and dulling our higher imagination as to what a better future for all really means? What can we expect from our national leadership, a leadership that rarely, if ever, speaks of God or morality and whose example often leaves much to be desired. Should we not be asking that most Augustinian of questions: Are the barbarians prevailing?

In the spring of 2012, Speaker of the House John Boehner spoke with journalist Peggy Noonan about a variety of issues, and included these sobering thoughts about our leadership, specifically his House colleagues.

"We've got 435 members here—It's just a slice of America, it really is. We've got some of the smartest people in the country who serve here, and some of the dumbest. We've got some of the best people you'd ever meet, and some of the raunchiest. We've got 'em all."[288]

As for scandals brewing, Boehner says, "I hear everything. There are no secrets in this town." And in his time (Boehner has twenty-four years in Congress), Noonan asks: "Has congressional misbehavior, publicly known or not, tended to go under the broadly defined category of "romance" or of "finance?" A long sigh, says Noonan. "Rarely is money an issue," says Boehner.[289]

Another example: Vice President Joe Biden, during the 2012 presidential campaign, was asked on national television about his position on same-sex marriage. Biden, a Catholic, responded that he is "absolutely comfortable" with gay marriage. "The bottom line on these issues is: Are they in love?" Not much of an argument there for our most fundamental, time-honored institution. Seems to be all about ardor, comfort—whatever—couched in new levels of expedient morality.

Then of course there is President Obama and his "evolving position." Publicly, at least, he once shared the position of his opponent that marriage should be between one man and one woman. Back in 2004, when he was asked, "What in (his) religious faith calls (him) to be against gay marriage?" he stated, "What I believe, in my faith, is that a man and a woman, when they get married, are performing something before God, and it's not simply the two persons who are meeting." Although the president believed in civil unions back then, he was clear that marriage should be preserved as God's model for marriage.[290]

By May 9, 2012, his "attitude"—his word choice — had evolved, "because I have a whole host of friends who are in gay partnerships.

I have staff members who are in committed monogamous relationships, who are raising children, who are wonderful parents. Therefore, for me personally, it is important to go ahead and affirm that I think same-sex couples should be able to get married."[291]

One feels compelled to ask: Given this evolving approach, why support even 'monogamous' relationships? Aren't they evolving too? Indeed ... isn't everything? So much for natural law. So much for moral absolutes. So much for thousands of years of tradition among every conceivable culture as to the relationship of marriage, procreation and family. So much, indeed, for Christianity.

Regarding gay rights, following a trend of nearly ten years with *Romer v. Evans* in 1996 on gay rights in Colorado, followed by *Lawrence v. Texas* in 2003 on the laws on sodomy, the tipping point on gay rights was the Supreme Judicial Court in Massachusetts in 2003 and 2004 installing same-sex marriage as nothing less than a constitutional right.

"These were the moves that drove the culture war over the edge," writes Professor Hadley Arkes. "More than anything else, that matter of gay marriage established the hegemony of the Left in the culture and in our politics, as we found that we could not break the hold of the courts and their allies in the political class, sustained by the media and the 'best schools' in the country."[292]

The Need for Vision

We are indeed losing space in the public square for the Christian and Catholic vision of which Cardinal Ratzinger speaks. A vision, said Ratzinger, which risks becoming something purely private and essentially mutilated. "We must defend religious freedom against the imposition of an ideology that presents itself as the only voice of rationality."[293]

Despite their intellectual pedigrees, perhaps the President and his colleagues can't relate to our religious heritage because of ignorance. Perhaps they are unaware that philosophical protagonists of classical liberalism, (vs. today's socialized version) —men such as Locke, Jefferson, Kant — whatever their interpretations of the Bible, were nonetheless inspired by Christianity.

Marcello Pera, a political professor and former president of the Italian Senate, makes a complimentary critical point in his book, *Why We Should Call Ourselves Christians* (the preface to which was written by Pope Benedict XVI). "Without faith in the equality, dignity, liberty and responsibility of all men," writes Pera, "that is to say, without a religion of man as the son and image of God (which is the essence of Judeo-Christian religion), liberalism cannot defend the fundamental and universal rights of human beings or hope that human beings can coexist in a liberal society."

"A condition is necessary," says Pera, "if liberals are to preserve the core of their doctrine. Basic human rights must be seen as a gift of God, to use Jefferson's phrase."[294]

By 'liberalism' here Pera means 'old liberalism,' the now misplaced liberal belief in the moral and rational unity of mankind and of natural rights: "all human beings are free and equal by nature; their basic liberties exist prior to and independent of the state, and are non-coercible by the state."[295]

He also means a liberalism that once acknowledged its historical and conceptual ties to Christianity, versus the current version that says religion should not voice opinions, that it is irrelevant to public life, that it is outmoded in the modern world, etc. He means a modern liberal world, as Russell Kirk wrote in the *New York Times* in 1956, which is "making its way straight toward what C.S. Lewis called 'the abolition of man.'"

As for Locke, Kant and Jefferson, Pera points out that all "linked the fundamental rights of men and the foundation of the liberal state to the commandments of the Christian God." All three were 'anti-clerical' in their own ways but none of them was 'secular', 'agnostic', a 'nonbeliever', or an 'atheist' —all categories they would not have understood or would have rejected.

More than 100 years after Locke, as noted, Jefferson framed that rhetorical question: "Can the liberties of a nation be thought secure when we have removed their only firm basis, a conviction in the minds of the people that these liberties are the gift of God?"[296]

All of which is to say that the liberal ethos, at its vital core and in its origins, derived from the notion that we are God's children, created in His image. And that it is He, not the will of the people much less the state, who has given us truth and freedom and the loving duty to fulfill His will. And not for His good but for His glory and, reflectively, for ours.

What is the core of liberalism, a term much used and much misunderstood after all these years? The foundation of liberalism as understood by the fathers — men such as Locke and Jefferson— is the idea of natural rights, also known as human, fundamental, essential or basic rights. It is the idea that human rights are grounded in rationality, and that they are universal and inalienable.

It also means that every person is free to pursue his or her conception of the good. All enjoy freedom of conscience and of religion.[297]

This may sound relativistic because freedom is involved. Which is to say, we are not 'forced' or 'determined' to choose appropriate goods. We can *not choose* them ... in this sense, we are indeed, in a distinctive but relative way, free.

But classical liberalism is actually grounded, not just on freedom but on an ontologic (i.e., *absolute*) notion of 'goods' that, because of their existential weight, *should* be valued and pursued—they are inalienable, after all. And they are good for the person. But they can be rejected, as we so often see. That's what 'choice' is all about. Not only freedom from coercion but also freedom to choose the authentic, enduring good.

The key point here, of course—arguing against the 'new liberal' relativism and 'alienable' rights—is that goods are metaphysical, or, better said, *ontologic*. Which is to say they are rooted, not in choice but *in reality*. We don't 'create' the goods, we don't create the values, as the Founders saw so well, because *they precede us.*

We (hopefully) discover them (they are not all equivalent nor patently obvious), and we choose them or not. Not all choices are necessarily good choices, as the lessons of life aptly demonstrate. To deny this is to fall into a hopeless 'idealism' *nee* relativism that makes freedom an 'absolute' but without its needed corollary, the end or values or goods to be chosen.

Chapter Thirteen: Separation of Church and State

"The Constitution ... is a mere thing of wax in the hands of the judiciary, which they may twist and shape into any form they please." Thomas Jefferson

But where, one might ask, does this leave the important 'separation of Church and state' issue? It bears pointing out that Jefferson's famous phrase "separation between Church and State," does not appear in the First Amendment or the Constitution. Neither, in fact, mention "separation," "Church," or "state." The phrase appears in a letter he sent to Connecticut's Danbury Baptist Association in 1802—fourteen years after the First Amendment was passed by Congress— to thank them for an earlier greeting and to reaffirm the language of the Amendment.

First Amendment

So what does the First Amendment say? The First Amendment's opening sixteen words stipulate that "Congress shall make no law respecting an establishment of religion, or prohibiting the free exercise thereof." The "establishment" phrase was important because the new states in the 1790s exhibited exceptional religious diversity. Indeed, Americans then seemed more fascinated than worried about religious diversity.

In 1784, for example, Hannah Adams, a distant cousin of John Adams, found a huge audience for her book *"Alphabetical Compendium of the Various Sects which have appeared in the World from the Beginning of the Christian Era to the Present Day."*[298]

Jefferson actually participated in none of the First Amendment debates. He was in France at the time the Bill of Rights was passed by Congress and ratified by the States. Nor do his own views and actions reconcile with the strict separation of state and religion interpretation often attributed to him.

During Jefferson's presidency, for example, Congress approved the use of the Capitol building as a church building for Christian worship services, which Jefferson attended on Sundays. He approved of paid government musicians to assist at these services. He also approved of similar worship services in his own Executive Branch, both at the Treasury Building and at the War Office.

There is ample evidence as to the extent to which federal facilities — supported by Jefferson —were placed at the disposal of religion after the Founders moved the government to Washington in 1800. Such that James H. Hutson, curator of the Library of Congress exhibition in 1998, *Religion and the Founding of the American Republic,* said that on Sundays during the first years in Washington, "the state became the Church."[299]

Later, when Jefferson founded the University of Virginia, he designated space in its rotunda for chapel services and indicated he expected students to attend these weekly services.[300]

As for Jefferson and the Baptists, the issue was not religion—at least twenty-five different versions of Christianity plus Judaism and Islam abounded at that time—but establishment. And the 'establishment' issue for eighteenth-century America was not advancement of religion, as modern jurisprudence would suggest, but Anglican control.

In England, it was the state that controlled the Church, not the Church that controlled the state. An array of parliamentary laws punished Catholics, Puritans and Quakers who attempted to openly exercise their religious faith outside of the official Church.[301]

Three days after Jefferson wrote the Danbury letter, he attended church in the largest congregation in North America at the time. This church held its weekly worship services on government property, in the House Chambers of the U.S. Capitol Building, and Jefferson was to attend these services consistently for the next seven years.[302]

The symbolism of Jefferson's actions corresponds with the rhetoric of his fellow Founders. Separation was meant to keep government out of religion, not religion out of public life. Evidently, the wall of separation against religion in 1802 could not be constructed anywhere in the country, not even on government property.

This is how it is written in the Constitution, this is how Thomas Jefferson understood it from his letter and actions, and this is how the men who wrote the Constitution practiced it. Jefferson once put it this way: "The First Amendment has created a wall of separation between the Church and the State. But that wall is one directional. It is to keep the government from running the Church. But it is not to keep Christian principles out of the government."[303]

As to how we got to our present place as a 'naked public square'— abandoning our religious roots in favor of becoming a secularized state and culture— a leading contemporary scholar on the issue, Philip Hamburger, has this to say:

"There is much reason to believe that the modern suppositions about the wisdom and influence of Jefferson's words regarding separation have developed largely as part of a twentieth-century myth — an account that has become popular precisely because *it has seemed to provide* constitutional authority for separation."[304]

Keeping principles of Christianity in rather than out of government is reflected in many of the concepts and guarantees of the Northwest Ordinance of 1787, for example, which antedated the First Amendment and were incorporated in the Constitution and the Bill of Rights. In the Northwest Territory, religious tolerance was proclaimed, and it was enunciated that "religion, morality, and knowledge, being necessary to good government and the happiness of mankind, schools and the means of education shall *forever be encouraged.*" [305] (emphasis added)

Paul Johnson, while acknowledging Jefferson's deism, has also called him a "closet theologian," who read daily from a multilingual edition of the New Testament.[306] Notwithstanding his deism and that of James Madison (both Christians who paid homage to the Bible), and Franklin's "role model" view of Christ, Protestant Christianity in its various sects was by far the dominant religion in America at its founding.

So it's abundantly clear what religion was being protected by the Fathers. Further support of this point is that both Jefferson and Franklin— the two most deist Founders—proposed Biblical images for the great seal of the United States (themes from the *Exodus* in both instances).[307]

As for Franklin, whatever his ambivalence toward Christianity, he was not indifferent to its tenets. He saw a strong connection between civic virtue and religious virtue. He once wrote to his wife, "God is very good to us." "Let us ... show our sense of His goodness to us by continuing to do good to our fellow creatures."[308]

In his earlier years as an industrious printer, Franklin became quite enamored with the aforementioned, hugely popular roving preacher, George Whitefield. He published accounts of Whitefield's appearances in forty-five weekly issues of his *Gazette*, and eight times turned over his entire front page to reprints of his sermons.

Franklin was obviously captivated by the transforming effect of Whitefield's preaching on Philadelphia's citizenry. "Never did the people show so great a willingness to attend sermons," he reported in the *Gazette*. "Religion is become the subject of most conversations. No books are in request but those of piety."[309]

It was also Franklin who, during a particularly contentious period over state's representations in the new government in 1787, asked that the Constitutional Convention begin each day's session with prayers. At the end of his life, the eighty-one-year-old Franklin asserted that "the longer I live, the more convincing proofs I see of this Truth—that God governs in the Affairs of Men." "I also believe," he continued, that "without his concurring Aid, we shall succeed in this political Building no better than the Builders of Babel."[310]

When contemporary sociologist Robert Bellah engages the issue of Church and state and its presumptive separation, he asks some penetrating questions, including, in these secularized times, "how is a president justified in using the word 'God' at all?"[311] His response is that separation of Church and state does not deny the political realm a religious dimension.

As he puts it:

> "Matters of personal religious belief, worship, and association are considered to be strictly private affairs, there are, at the same time, certain common elements of religious orientation that the great majority of Americans share. These have played a crucial role in the development of American institutions and still provide a religious dimension for the whole fabric of American life, including the political sphere.

> "This public religious dimension is expressed in a set of beliefs, symbols, and rituals that I am calling American civil religion. The inauguration of a president is an important ceremonial event in this religion. It reaffirms, among other things, the religious legitimization of the highest political authority."[312]

The question for Bellah would seem to be: If matters of personal religious belief and worship are to be considered *strictly* private affairs that, when exercised, have minimal ramifications on the public order, are we not left with a much-diminished God, and a tragically diminished man?

What then has happened to Providence? And what has happened to community? After all, to paraphrase Aristotle, man is by nature *social.* What he believes, and what he does, inevitably impacts others. The fact is, as we have shown, the Founders emphasized that government should not prevent the free exercise of religion in part because *they saw the value of personal religious belief to the public order.* Indeed, they wanted to *encourage* religious belief, as held by individuals, to be present in communal life and constitute an integral part of the American democratic way of life.

The value of this connection between the state and personal religious practice persisted long after the founding period. Justice Joseph Story, in his *Familiar Exposition of the Constitution,* completed in 1840 and designed for students in the common schools and academies of Massachusetts, maintained it was the "general, if not universal sentiment in America ... that Christianity ought to receive encouragement from the state, so far as was not incompatible with the private rights of conscience, and the freedom of religious worship. An attempt to level all religions, and to make it a matter of state policy to hold all in utter indifference, would have created universal disapprobation, if not universal indignation." [313]

Judicial Power and Separation

Jefferson had presciently warned against the power of the judiciary in altering the intent of the Founders and the Constitution. He wrote on September 6, 1819, "The Constitution ... is a mere thing of wax in the hands of the judiciary, which they may twist and shape into any form they please."[314]

And, of course, it happened, as in 1947 in *Everson v. Board of Education,* when the Supreme Court for the first time interpreted the "separation" phrase as requiring the federal government to remove religious expressions from the public arena. That is, it interpreted the First Amendment, not as a limitation on government interference, but rather as a limitation on religious expressions and principles!

That Court, unlike previous ones, did not reprint Jefferson's Danbury letter. It merely used eight words from the letter and did not give the context of the phrase, or mention Jefferson's numerous other statements on the subject. Nor did it mention that previous Supreme Courts had used Jefferson's letter to preserve religious principles in public society. In short, that 1947 Court was the first to divorce Jefferson's metaphor from its context and then applied it *exactly opposite* to Jefferson's clearly articulated intent.

Given the very prominent role of Supreme Court Justice Hugo Black in writing this decision, a brief review of his background would appear in order. Black was a Baptist from Alabama, a progressive New Dealer who ran for the Senate in 1925 and 1926 by appealing to the "Dry-Protestant-Progressive" voters in the state. He was also a Mason considerably influenced by the anti-Catholic Southern Jurisdiction of Scottish Rite Masons. (In the late 1940s, at least seven justices of the Supreme Court belonged to one Masonic organization or another, three being attached to the Southern Jurisdiction of the Scottish Rite.)[315]

Black had also been a member of the Ku Klux Klan and gained some notoriety in 1921 by defending a Klansman against a charge of murder of a Catholic priest. The Klan provided Black with his path to the Senate. In September, Black joined the powerful Richard E. Lee Klan No. 1 and promptly became Kladd of the Klavern —the officer who initiated new members by administering the oath about "white supremacy" and "separation of Church and State."[316]

After his election, Imperial Wizard Hiram Evans awarded Black the very rare honor of a golden "grand passport." It wasn't until 1937, when Black's association with the Klan became public, that President Franklin Delano Roosevelt, disavowing awareness of his former Klan membership, appointed Black as Associate Justice of the Supreme Court, much to the horror of many Americans, not least, Catholics.

In 1925, in *Pierce v. Society of Sisters*, the Supreme Court struck down an Oregon law (adopted by initiative) that in effect outlawed private schools. This was a pet project of the Ku Klux Klan and was blatantly anti-Catholic.[317]

It was Black's opinion, written for the majority in *Everson v. Board of Education,* which said the clause against establishment of religion was intended to erect "a wall of separation between Church and State." And in so doing, it bears pointing out, substituted the judicial for the amendment process. Going forward, the opinion in Everson would become the foundation of constitutional jurisprudence in the United States on the separation of Church and state. And, it must be added, with no small effect upon the separation of faith and loss of soul from public life as well.

Several years later Everson was reinforced in the *McCollum v. Board of Education* case (1948), when the Supreme Court —with Black again writing the majority opinion — declared that religious instruction on public school premises was contrary to the Constitution. This decision dismayed many Protestants, bringing them to "recognize that they faced a greater threat from secularism and separation than from Catholicism.[318]

All of which prompted Peter Drucker to write, "the way we have handled the problem in the few cases that have come up so far is nothing to be proud of. I am convinced that it is a thoroughly untenable decision on ordinary legal grounds."[319]

Drucker's point here is that to rule it unconstitutional for a school district to grant "released time" for religious instruction (because to do so interfered with the religious freedom of an atheist schoolchild), represented an absurdity and is in clear violation of the Constitution's mandate against preventing free exercise. It meant the phrase in the Constitution that forbids Congress to make a law respecting an establishment of religion (a denominational issue) actually means forbidding the *practice* of religion.

It further means the federal government actually *controls* the question of religion —more specifically the practice of religion, misrepresented as establishment—anywhere in the States. One might add that the ruling doesn't do much for protecting the 'free exercise' clause either.

It is also interesting to note just what is being 'protected' in this decision, namely the freedom of non-belief of an atheist, which, in fact, is not in question or in jeopardy. Nothing is forbidding the child from continuing his non-belief. Nor is it protection against establishment of a religion, but against the practice of religion, which is what the First Amendment specifically *encourages*!

It is not hard to see where all this leads, contra to the thinking, practice and wishes of the Founders and generations of their philosophical disciples. Namely to an institutionalized, judicially supported bias *against* the practice of religion— and a massive step forward towards the practical separation of faith from culture in America.

Drucker notes further that the most important point here is not the constitutional one. The more significant point is that the American creed recognized and protected a secular state but presupposed a religious society. And that the "free exercise" clause was a positive policy of impartial encouragement of all religious life and activity in American society, which the Founders respected and wished to promote.

Prof. Lawrence Friedman of Yale observes that, at present, "Religion has politely been shown the door. Indeed many religious parents are disturbed because the schools are now so godless. The schools teach evolution. They ban prayers and Bible reading. They teach nothing about religion. This makes them enemies of religion." As for making school "neutral," Friedman says it is, "strictly speaking, a mirage. Even science is an ideology. As of 2001, the public schools ignore religion, one of the most powerful social forces in the world."[320]

(It is unfortunate in the extreme, when young students are massacred in the presumed protective environment of their schools, that the remedial discussions focus on the instrument of their deaths—and the legal remedies—rather than the moral and cultural neutrality that, in effect, has ignored the moral instruction of our young people for generations.)

As for what this moral neutrality represents for the public square, Friedman makes the compelling observation that it is "the master change in the general culture in the twentieth century: *the triumph of the individual, the exaltation of the self.*"[321]

Jacques Maritain, in his intellectual style, might refer to this as "egregious anthropocentrism," or "anarchical individualism," or even, in its most tragic form, a "satanocentrism."[322]

In another place, he calls such moral neutrality: "bourgeois liberalism, whose pretension it is to base everything on the individual

161

considered as a little god, and on his caprice, on the absolute liberty of property, of commerce, and of the pleasures of life," a liberalism which ends *in etatisme,* the hypertrophy and absolute primacy of the State."[323]

An important Supreme Court decision in 1962 —by now the liberal Warren Court— illustrates how the separation issue had come full circle to become a prohibition issue. The case was *Engel v. Vitale,* and the issue was how far public schools could go to promote religion. Schools at one time had not been at all bashful about religion; they assigned Bible reading and conducted prayers in schools. But by the 1960s, and with new legal precedent, that had dramatically changed.

Engel concerned the so-called Regents prayer, whereby the New York Board of Regents composed a (presumably) bland enough and non-denominational enough prayer for classroom recitation. It read: "Almighty God, we acknowledge our dependence upon Thee, and beg Thy blessings upon us, our parents, our teachers and our Country."[324]

This was not bland enough for the American Civil Liberties Union, the American Jewish Committee, or the Supreme Court itself. Quite ignoring the religious sentiments of the founding fathers, not to mention Abraham Lincoln, Franklin Roosevelt, Harry Truman, John Kennedy, Ronald Reagan et al., the Court said it was "no part of the business of government ... to compose official prayers," much less have them read in school. [325]

A year later, the Court struck down a Pennsylvania law that ordered public schools to read ten verses from the Bible aloud each day in class. This too was an "establishment of religion" and therefore unconstitutional.

Hardly any decisions of the Court have been less popular than the school prayer decisions, yet the Court has clung stubbornly to its 'principles' and has in fact extended the doctrine. In response, numerous amendments to the Constitution to allow prayers in school have been proposed over the years — President Ronald Reagan was one of the proposers — but none have gotten much past the starting gate.[326]

The ambiguity of all this, especially given the well-defined intent of the First Amendment to *not prohibit* the free exercise of religion, is no doubt why former Chief Justice of the U.S. Supreme Court William Rehnquist said, "The metaphor of a wall of separation is bad history and worse law. It has made a positive chaos out of court rulings. It should be explicitly abandoned."[327]

This is in rather stark contrast to the separationist and secularist position held by Stephen Breyer, Ruth Bader Ginsburg and retired Justice David Souter of the U.S. Supreme Court, who claim the establishment clause prevents any government endorsement or support of religious practices. An exaggerated distinction of Church from state, needless to say, that is promoting the separation of faith from daily life the founding fathers so clearly abhorred.

As mentioned, by 1947, in *Everson v. Board of Education*, the establishment clause was interpreted to apply against the states. It was not until the middle to late twentieth century, however, that the Supreme Court began to interpret the establishment and free exercise clauses so as to actually *restrict* the promotion of religion by the states. Coming full circle from the Founders' intent, Justice Souter, writing for the majority in the *Board of Education of Kiryas Joel Village School District v. Grumet* (1994), concluded that "government should not prefer one religion to another, *or religion to irreligion*."[328]

Meaning that religious indifferentism had been taken to a new level in this country, a level of enshrinement. So much for our national currency and "In God We Trust." So much for the Pledge of Allegiance. So much for Patrick Henry's famous quote, "It cannot be emphasized too strongly or too often that this great nation was founded not by religion but by Christians, not on religions but on the Gospel of Jesus Christ." And yes, so much for the clear intentions of the Founders. Communism, at least, was overtly atheistic.

All of which says that not only shall a single denomination not prevail in America, but also that government has spoken on religion itself in a whole new light. Namely on the equivalency of believing in God —and not believing in God, per Justice Souter. The government of the people —91 percent of whom supported amending the *Pledge of Allegiance* to include the phrase "under God" in 1954—is thus officially indifferent to the mores (and the behavior that follows upon belief) of its people, as well as to its cultural soul. To what or whether the people believe or don't believe and to whether religious belief plays any role in governance or in public life.

Which is also to say that the people themselves, whom the government represents and who are generally religious —the vast majority of Americans believe in God and three quarters of them declare themselves Christian—should not be concerned as to whether their government is supportive or not of these beliefs.[329] So much for Lincoln's government "of, by and for the people."

Other Supreme Court Decisions

Meanwhile— in a manner of speaking— other relevant Supreme Court decisions in support of the *Everson* position were forthcoming. As mentioned, there is *Engel v. Vitale* (1962), saying "Any kind of prayer, composed by public school districts, even nondenominational prayer, is unconstitutional government sponsorship of religion."

There is *Abington School District v. Schempp* (1963), where the "Court finds Bible reading over school intercom unconstitutional"— although the Court did concede in Schempp "that the Founding Fathers believed devotedly that there was a God and (that) the unalienable rights of man were rooted in Him is clearly evidenced in their writings, from the Mayflower Compact to the Constitution itself." And there is *Murray v. Curlett* (1963), "Court finds forcing a child to participate in Bible reading and prayer unconstitutional."

It was not always so. The Supreme Court has said —repeatedly— that the religion clauses of the First Amendment are heavily grounded in the history surrounding their adoption, and it is a rich and full history, "yet, throughout much of the modern Establishment Clause jurisprudence the courts have largely ignored this history. Instead, they have abridged this history and focused almost single-mindedly on only one figure—Thomas Jefferson — and only one concept — the 'wall of separation.'" [330]

For a real head-scratcher regarding our highest Court, one need only consider the decision in *Stone v. Graham* in 1980, where the Supreme Court held that Kentucky schools could not display the Ten Commandments on classroom walls because: "if posted copies of the Ten Commandments are to have any effect at all, it will be to induce the schoolchildren to read, meditate upon, perhaps to venerate and obey, the Commandments," which, the Court said, is "not a permissible state objective under the Establishment Clause." One can only wonder what the parents of the Columbine and Newtown children think of such juridical non-sense.

Apparently the architects and designers of the Supreme Court building, built in 1935, did not foresee *Stone v. Graham*. There are, throughout the Supreme Court's building, numerous representations of the Ten Commandments, and Moses.[331] Nor did the architects neglect the National Archives, home of our nation's most important documents. Its entrance has an image of the Ten Commandments engraved in bronze on its floor.

Indeed, as Newt Gingrich's inspiring book, *Rediscovering God in America* notes, a simple walking tour of our nation's capital gives ample example, both on parchment and "literally written into the rock, mortar and marble of American history" of the belief that "our Creator is the source of American liberty." Near the end of his book, Gingrich quotes the conclusion of President John Kennedy's inaugural in 1961:

> "With a good conscience our only sure reward, with history the final judge of our deeds, let us go forth to lead the land we love, asking His blessing and His help but knowing that here on earth, God's work must truly be our own."

Gingrich's closing chapter notes the Latin words *Laus Deo* ("Praise be to God"). They appear on the eastern side of our capital's tallest building, the monument dedicated to the father of our country, George Washington.[332]

The *Wall Street Journal* (October 2, 2012) presented an example of how far constitutional re-wiring has come to confuse "establishment" versus "exercise" in the United States. That is the case of a Texas public high school cheerleading squad, brought to court to find out if it can hoist banners inscribed with biblical verses during football games. One banner read: "But thanks be to God, which gives us Victory, through our Lord Jesus Christ." (1 Cor.15:57)

The Freedom from Religion Foundation in Madison, Wisconsin, found out about this "transgression of freedom," and, after complaining, the Kountze, Texas, schools' superintendent banned the signs. The legal issue was expected to revolve on whether the banners are seen as endorsed by the school (presumably this would mean "establishment" rather than "free exercise") or only as representing the cheerleaders' personal beliefs.

A professor of constitutional law at the University of Virginia School of Law, Douglas Laycock, apparently does not see this as either a censorship issue or a 'free exercise' issue. "I do not think there is much doubt that it is unconstitutional," he says, since this is "very specifically Christian and clearly sponsored by the school," even though no school officials were involved with the cheerleaders' decision to make the banners.[333]

Heaven forbid, in these secular times, some inspiring religion working its way —via students no less—on to a high school football field in predominately Christian Texas. This hardly seems like "establishment," especially given that no Christian denomination is mentioned or encouraged. On the other hand, the ban strikes one as clearly preventing "free exercise," which, once again, is what our Founders felt the need to promote.

In a later development on this issue, at least a little (non-denominational) Christianity is still alive in Texas. Texas state district judge Steve Thomas ruled in May 2013 that the cheerleaders may display banners with Bible verses at football games. The judge determined the banners are constitutionally permissible, noting that no law "prohibits cheerleaders from using religious-themed banners at school sporting events."[334]

The Plano, Texas, law firm representing the cheerleaders argued that the girls' free-speech rights were being violated. The cheerleaders in Kountze, about ninety-five miles northeast of Houston, were supported by various state officials.

The school district, which received a complaint about the banners from the Freedom from Religion Foundation, argued the banners violated a First Amendment clause that bars government —or publicly funded school districts —from establishing or endorsing a religion. Again, quite lost in these judicial machinations, is the First Amendment trying, as has been repeatedly noted, to protect *the free exercise of religion.*

Maritain on America and Separation

Jacques Maritain was a French Thomistic philosopher who, by his own admission, had the good fortune to spend many years in the United States and came to deeply love this country, as reflected in his gracious book, *Reflections on America.* Maritain wrote extensively on Church and state matters, and, as a great thinker and a European, had keen insights on the separation issue and on the American experiment in general.

As he insightfully noted:

> "... the expression 'separation between Church and State,' which in itself is a misleading expression, does not have the same meaning here and in Europe. In Europe it means, or it meant, that complete isolation which derives from century-old misunderstandings and struggles, and which has produced most unfortunate results.

"Here it means, as a matter of fact, together with a refusal to grant any privilege to one religious denomination in preference to others and to have a State established religion, a distinction between the State and the Churches which is compatible with good feeling and mutual cooperation. Sharp distinction and actual cooperation, that's a historical treasure—Please to God that you keep it carefully, and not let your concept of separation veer around to the European one."[335]

As for the historical and evangelical roots of the U.S. Constitution, Maritain had this to say:

"The Constitution of this country is deep-rooted in the age-old heritage of Christian thought and civilization. As I put it in *Scholasticism and Politics,* 'its structure owes little to Rousseau, if I am to believe some Dominican friends of mine that this Constitution has rather some relation to ideas which presided in the Middle Ages at the constitution of St. Dominic's Order ...'"

And he continued:

"Peerless is the significance, for political philosophy, of the establishment of the American Constitution at the end of the 18th century. This Constitution can be described as an outstanding lay Christian document tinged with the philosophy of the day. The spirit and inspiration of this great political Christian document is *basically repugnant to the idea of making human society stand aloof from God and from any religious faith.* (emphasis added) "Thanksgiving and public prayer, the invocation of the name of God at the occasion of any major official gathering, are, in the practical behavior of the nation, a token of this very same spirit and inspiration."[336]

Denominational Christianity versus 'Christian by inspiration'

Great thinker that he is, and deeply aware of his Christian history and of the separation issue in America, Jacques Maritain helps clarify the Church-state issue with a vital distinction. Namely that which is 'denominationally Christian' versus that which is 'Christian by inspiration.'

These distinctions are especially relevant to our discussion over the proper meaning of separation between Church and state in a society that is predominately Christian but comprised of many different Christian sects. The Founders were obviously concerned with 'denominational Christianity,' in that they did not favor establishment of one particular denomination in America.

At the same time, they were faced with the challenge of preserving a "Christian nation," as it was often referred to, and with its corresponding belief in God and in a moral order and codes of behavior. Which is to say, they wanted a nation that was socially and culturally "inspired" by Christianity.

The solution to this challenge, of course, was in the notion of separation of Church and state. That meant that the state could not impose its view as to a preferred Christian sect, while at the same time it was prohibited from passing any legislation that would prevent religious practice. In spite of the obfuscations and confusion wrought by the judicial interpretations of the amendment over the years, this is clearly what the First Amendment says.

Maritain, a Frenchman, is a great admirer of America. He believes the American Constitution is providential in that it correctly embraces the notion of separation of Church from state while also enabling it to encourage religious practice personally and collectively, and expecting appropriate social and cultural benefits from this practice. This is to say that Church and state are definitely *distinct* from one another and autonomous in their own orders. But, since their constituencies are— at one and the same time— of both orders, they are not, de facto, *separate*.

But how then, we might ask, do the benefits of religion accrue to the state? They do not do so by virtue of law or by preferred status, but by virtue of influence, mores, personal behavior and cultural enlightenment. This is what, I suggest, Maritain believes by the notion of "Christian by inspiration." He means that the social, political and cultural orders— and economic as well —are not meant to be directly guided by a specific Christian denomination, but that they are —positively or negatively —affected by how well their denominations' adherents live up to the tenets of their faith. And the positive law emanating from such a society will reflect these tenets.

As for participation in this grand task of elevating all of the temporal order, it should not be understood as an exclusively Christian task but a task for all of good heart, Christian or not. As reflected in the Catholic Church's teaching in *Gaudium et Spes* (Vatican II), for example, the explanation of the "mystery of man" — rooted in the mystery of the Incarnate Word—

"holds true not for Christians only *but also for all men of good will* in whose hearts grace is active invisibly.

"For since Christ died for all, and since all men are in fact called to one and the same destiny, which is divine, we must hold that the Holy Spirit *offers to all* the possibility of being made partners, in a way known to God, in the Paschal Mystery."[337] (emphases added)

Chapter Fourteen: The Larger Issue— Separation of Faith and Culture

"... the society or culture which has lost its spiritual roots is a dying culture, however prosperous it may appear externally." Christopher Dawson

Christopher Dawson, the eminent Christian historian of religion and culture, saw the great challenge of our time this way:

> "The central conviction which has dominated my mind ever since I began to write is the conviction that the society or culture which has lost its spiritual roots is a dying culture, however prosperous it may appear externally. Consequently the problem of social survival is not only a political or economic one; it is above all things religious, since it is in religion that the ultimate spiritual roots both of society and the individual are to be found."[338]

These words from a learned historian reflect a studied conviction that is not unlike that of the founding fathers of this country, which is that this society—and this country — *need* religion. They saw what Dawson wrote so extensively about; namely that the body politic, like the body itself, is incomplete and possibly even dead without a soul. That 'soul' is religion, which is why it is not to be mandated, but protected and nurtured.

"In the last resort," wrote Dawson, "every civilization is built on a religious foundation: it is the expression in social institutions and cultural activity of a faith or vision of reality which gives the civilization its spiritual unity. Thus the great world cultures correspond with the great world religions and when a religion dies the civilization that it inspired gradually decays."[339]

Modernity's Great Challenge: Relativism

As for the great challenge of relativism today, let's first attempt to define it. Setting aside all intellectual obfuscation and 'ideosophy,' at its core relativism says there are no true absolutes and no single true morality. Indeed, there are no inalienable rights, hence all things are relative. (Saying this absolutely while denying absolutes is a confounding question, to be sure!)

Consequently, for the relativist, there are many different moral frameworks from which to operate. None is more correct or more 'true' than the others. There are no 'commandments.' At the end of the day, there may be conventions, but there is no truth.

As a result, we can say that for the relativist: (1) moral truth does not exist; (2) there is no common scale of values by which we may measure diverse values; (3) transcultural and trans-historical values do not exist; and (4) there is no solution to value conflicts that is universally valid.

A Key Challenge to Democracy: Exaltation of the Self

If on the philosophical level —the level of ideas —the key challenge to democracy is relativism (whatever we all vote on is true!)— on the personal level this relativism typically translates into some form of egoism. (After all, if all values are relative, why not make oneself the key value?)

It can be argued that this 'practical relativism,' needing some locus and often finding it in the great but subjective forces of Protestantism, typically points to making the self the definer of values and the focal point of life. One might call it "the exaltation or deification of the self" or "relativism in action."

One of the great problems with this approach on the social level, of course, is that it is 'non-communal' and not highly supportive of democracy. It can easily disregard the common good by putting its own welfare before that of others. If it can be said that man cannot live without love, then this is the self-absorbed love of the practical relativist.

This challenge to recognize 'the other,' and in some real way to prioritize the other, has its roots much deeper than does democracy. It has biblical roots; it represents the primeval challenge faced by the First Parents. That, of course, was the disobedience in the Garden, the first putting of self before Other, and the first rejection of law and of principle.

The Romantic and Idealist reaction to Locke, Kant, Aquinas, Aristotle, and those who opted for principles common to all humanity, was to take the obvious (and only remaining) approach by saying that there is no single principle—metaphysical, ethical or rational—that can be binding on all humanity. There are only historical cultures, each with its own principles, values and hierarchies, or, in other words, multiculturalism— values *du jour*.

Thus we have Nietzsche saying, "Facts do not exist, only interpretations," and we have Derrida decreeing, "There is nothing outside the text," leading (logically!) to Feyerabend's famous slogan, "Anything goes," and we have Sartre saying, *a priori*, "There is no God!"[340]

A helping hand in understanding these matters is Cardinal Joseph Ratzinger (later Pope Benedict XVI) and his reflections on the famous Russian scientist and dissident, Andrei Sakharov, who had to live the insidiousness of relativism first hand. Ratzinger called him more than a great scientist. Sakharov "was a great man" who for the sake of the "humanity of man, of his ethical dignity and his freedom," accepted great suffering and persecution at the hands of the Soviet Communists in service to the truth.

Because of his enormous prestige and prominence, Sakharov was the voice and conscience of the Russian people for decades—and was completely shut down by a false ideology and regime that, as the Pope wrote, "drove people to apathy, weariness, and indifference, reducing them to external and internal poverty."[341] In other words, a life that was the antithesis of a "civilization of love," of which Pope Benedict has written so much, in large part because the ideology being followed was a lie.

The truth-seeking dissident Sakharov won out, but it is evident that the fight is far from over. The struggle for true human dignity —and authentic human rights —has moved closer to our shores. Cardinal Ratzinger wrote, "Under the rule of the Marxist parties, a number of risks to man took the form of concrete political forces that were destroying the human quality of life, and *I believe these risks continue to exist, albeit in another form.*"[342]

We see these risks, especially now in our culture, in terms of the ascendancy of subjectivism, consumerism, materialism and moral relativism, and the attacks on the most fundamental, God- given (and very ancient) institutions of marriage and family. Institutions that go back to the dawning of civilization—thousands of years, in Egypt, in Rome, in Greece, in China —and which modernity now seems to find outdated.

Cardinal Ratzinger mentions the example of the American philosopher Richard Rorty, who has done much to formulate this "new utopia of banality." Fr. Richard Neuhaus's book, *American Babylon,* points out Rorty's claim that "we can say nothing about 'reality', about what is 'out there'—or at least nothing to which it is appropriate to attach terms such as 'true' or 'false'." [343]

"Rorty's ideal," says Ratzinger, "is a liberal society in which absolute values and criteria will no longer exist; a sense of well-being will be the only goal worth striving for." Ratzinger points out that Sakharov, based on his experience with the hollowing effect of Communism, anticipated the danger to the Western world from the "emptying-out" and devaluing of what is authentically human by bad ideas.

In our naiveté and cynicism, says Sakharov, we in America are neglecting our moral responsibilities, namely to protect a genuine freedom that is grounded in ethical foundations and absolute values. In truth, in the authentic good, and in law. As Cardinal Ratzinger put it, "We might say that freedom entails the ability of conscience to perceive the fundamental value of humanity, a value that concerns every individual."[344]

Ratzinger continues: "Freedom demands that governments and all those who bear responsibility bow down before a reality that is defenseless and incapable of exercising any coercion: *morality*." Of great concern to Ratzinger is that modern democracies, given over to the will of the majority, can accord validity to moral values that are not authentic, or that are not even sustained by the conviction of the majority.[345]

This was precisely Lincoln's concern in his famous debates with Stephen Douglas over the use of popular sovereignty to determine the future of slavery, vs. the greater issue of the immorality of slavery. Douglas said: *Let the people decide.* Lincoln said: *There is nothing to 'decide'...there is an absolute value here ... slavery is immoral!*

Rorty, if he were consistent with himself — he often is not—would permit slavery on this basis: the will of the majority. This can lead, as Lincoln clearly saw, to domination— the will (in this case of the people) made superior to reason, and the truth sacrificed to power.

The problem with the freedoms thus protected, and the challenge of getting everyone to live together, must therefore be based on the moral and rational unity of mankind — the brotherhood of man under the fatherhood of God. This, in turn, is a brotherhood underwritten, protected and inspired by Christian values, which were meant to provide the soul to society. The Founders believed in rigorous law; they also clearly saw a 'lived Christianity' as society's moral glue.

Given the lightweight, politically correct approaches to civics today (a Harvard and Stanford grad noted in the *Wall Street Journal* that the dominant intellectual culture at both schools "provided scant leadership in educating students about the foundation of freedom in the Western world, or even in promoting an understanding of the founding principles of our own nation"), it's not too surprising President Obama's team either never knew, or has forgotten, our authentic intellectual heritage.[346]

More likely they remember Jesse Jackson at Stanford in the late '80s and chants of "Hey, hey, ho, ho, Western culture's got to go."[347]

From a quantitative standpoint, religion— and specifically Christianity—should still make a strong case as our foundational value base. As noted, Christianity is "the largest and most popular religion in the United States, with around 77% of those polled identifying themselves as Christian as of 2009." Wikipedia further notes that in the mid 1990s, the United States had, with 224 million Christians, the largest Christian population on earth.[348]

As for our political leadership in Washington, nearly 90 percent of current members of Congress call themselves Christian, 30 percent of whom are Catholic—the largest denomination. Also of interest is that 98 percent of the members of the 113th Congress cite some specific religious affiliation.[349]

Whatever the numbers, however, the cultural slide towards moral neutrality and values *du jour* seems to continue unabated, suggesting that it is much more than a numbers game. Better to think of it as a "courage of conviction" game, based on recognizing— and generously living by—authentic and timeless values, both at home and in the public square.

A most helpful insight into how this is to be done is Karol Wojtyla's (later Pope John Paul II) remarkable study of the human person, particularly in his book *The Acting Person*. Here and elsewhere Wojtyla points out—in contrast to say Kant's absolutist "all moral laws have the character of being assented to by all rational creatures at all times in all cultures" — that human freedom, (i.e., living by moral norms), necessarily involves choice.[350]

And making choices, in turn, necessarily involves *the will*. The will is a dynamic faculty within the intellectual soul of every person, and is "the person's power of self-determination." This is not, he reminds us, the will acting alone and in "methodical isolation" but will as the indispensable "efficient cause" of the development of the whole person — the full realization of the human personality. [351]

The Drama of Contemporary Culture

The drama of contemporary culture, in the view of John Paul II, and more recently by Pope Francis in his apostolic exhortation "Evangelii Gaudium" (The Joy of the Gospel), is *materiality;* an insipid individuality and neglect of the infinite richness and destiny of the human personality. It results in a *lack of interiority*—a losing of oneself in the world outside; the banal, the trivial, the 'momentary,' the pleasurable—and an inability to *contemplate;* to fully relate to and make the higher values of goodness, of beauty, of truth, one's own.

Given the nature of the human person—who is the principal creator of culture—without the development of the 'inner self' culture has no content; it is like a body that has not found its soul. Or perhaps it *has* found its soul (John Paul II might say "its subjectivity"), and found it empty.

The lack of interiority of which John Paul II spoke at World Youth Day 2003 has profound personal as well as cultural ramifications. To deny oneself the proper development of one's own interiority — one's *subjectivity or inner life*—is to deny that which is most intimate, most creative, most expansive and most relational in the human person. Indeed, it is to deny what is most God-like in the person, who is made in His very image and who is therefore essentially "relational" and creative in every aspect of his being.

Indeed, to describe someone's personality is in fact an attempt to describe an interiority—a mystery-laden subjectivity— a "who" rather than a "what." Only a person is creative, expansive, reflective, dynamic and transcendent. Only a person is *imago Dei* and capable of an inner beauty, and of love. It is an attempt therefore, however haltingly, to reveal what is going on within a unique subject, which always has its limitations.

As soon as we resort to describing and defining we are *objectifying* the person, and trying to put into concepts and words what, by nature, transcend those very concepts and words. Whatever else might be said of the human person, at the core a person is a *mystery*, irreducible, beyond mere conceptualization and fully known to God alone.

And yet, given its enormous importance, the effort must be made to get at interiority —at *subjectivity*— at the rich inner life and specialness of the human person. Here it is helpful to reflect on Thomas Aquinas's *operatio sequitur esse*, i.e., "operations flow from the essence of the thing." Which is to say that while we cannot—in a literal way— see what's inside a person, we can know something of what a person is all about by what he or she *does*. By actions, or as Wojtyla puts it, by the *lived experience*.

"What can humanity do without interiority? Unfortunately, we know the answer very well. When the contemplative spirit is missing life is not protected and all that is human is denigrated." Without the exercise of interiority—the unique capacity of the human person to develop and form himself— "modern man puts his own integrity at risk."[352]

St. Augustine would surely have no problem with this observation, as even a cursory reading of his *Confessions* would quickly reveal. Nor would great protagonists of America's first Great Awakening; men such as Jonathan Edwards, George Whitefield and John Witherspoon, or, say, Charles Grandison Finney of the Second Awakening. All these men recognized the primacy of the spiritual and of the religious in the authentic development of America's citizens and of their country.

This is not, in any way, to denigrate creation or the material. As Dawson notes:

> "The essential achievement of our culture — the conquest of the material order — is not, as we have seen, inconsistent with this ideal (a true civilization, a true Christian culture). In fact it may be regarded as its natural complement, for the restoration of man to his true position as the master of nature and the organizer of the material world, which is the function of science, corresponds in the natural order to the spiritual restoration of human nature in itself, which is the world of Christianity in the supernatural order.

> "In a Christian civilization the scientific order would no longer offer, as it does at present, the tragic spectacle of vast resources of power and intelligence devoted to producing unsightly and unnecessary objects and to endowing mankind with new means of self-destruction; it would become an instrument for the realization of man's true destiny as the orderer of material things to spiritual ends.

"Without spiritual order the cosmopolitanism of modern culture does not make for peace; it merely increases the opportunities for strife. It destroys all that is best and most distinctive in the local and national cultures, while leaving the instincts of national and racial hostility to develop unchecked. It unites mankind in the common enjoyment of the cinema and the Ford car and the machine gun without creating any spiritual unity.

The recovery of the Christian idea of order would give a spiritual expression to the universality of modern culture. Its material unification would become subservient to the ideal of the spiritual unity of mankind in justice and charity, an ideal that has a very real attraction to the modern mind, but which secular idealism is powerless to achieve."[353]

Which is to say that the proper development of modern culture will require an "elevation of the spirit," an enriched interiority that can understand and embrace the eternal verities; realizing these verities are essentially dynamic, that they are born in the mind of a loving God, and that they are indispensable to nurturing a freedom-loving citizenry to a better future.

Chapter Fifteen: The Way Forward— Personal Humanism

"The human person is ... the fundamental subject of all social and political philosophy and at the very core of authentic democracy."
Jacques Maritain.

Perhaps no aspect of American history better dramatizes the issue of "personal humanism" or "theocentric humanism" as does the great Civil War. At issue, of course, was the notion of freedom, not as a philosophical abstraction but as a reality for millions of black Americans who were not — either in law or by practice— recognized as persons.

In fact, fully one-eighth of America's population in 1860 was in slavery and barely recognized even as individuals, much less citizens. Slaves were counted as three-fifths of a citizen for census and voting /representation purposes. But they were considered property, not people, and did not have the right to vote or any of the rights of citizens, the most precious of which, of course, is freedom.

Abraham Lincoln intuitively recognized that these nearly four million Americans —due to skin color—were not only being denied citizenship, but, more importantly, their rights and human dignity as children of God, as fellow citizens and as human persons. His famous debates with Stephen Douglas were precisely on this point, namely that a very substantial group of Americans were being grievously mistreated— morally and physically—and that it didn't matter how states coming into the Union felt about slavery, or how they voted.

Lincoln eloquently made the indispensable point, namely that morality is not determined by vote. Slavery, pure and simple, was a violation of natural rights, of personhood, and was, therefore, gravely wrong. It was not subject to individual votes because the dignity of the human person transcends individuality.

Despite the problems the Founders faced on the subject of slavery, this "person—individual" distinction is implicitly recognized in the protection they sought for freedom of conscience. So let us turn briefly to St. Thomas Aquinas, and then to Jacques Maritain, for a richer understanding of this all-important distinction.

The Human Person

The notion of the person—which has theological analogs of the highest order—has been a dynamic concept of great consequence, both philosophically and theologically, for centuries. It was already thoroughly examined by writers of the Patristic period, since most of the heresies in the early centuries of Christianity dealt with a faulty understanding of the mystery of the Trinity (three Persons in one God) and the mystery of the Incarnation (two natures in one Person). Aquinas makes the truly grand assertion that the person is the highest perfection in the created world. ("Heaven and earth shall pass away ...") The person is *perfectissumum ens* and *imago Dei*. The person is a 'self', an 'I' —a subsistent subject of existence and self-determining action—thus transcending the human being understood, as did the Aristotelean tradition, only as "an individual with a rational nature."

In the visible world, every human being is made in the image and likeness of God. This very unique being, for all its singularity and materiality, is objectively the most perfect and beautiful in all creation. It has an ultimate destiny that is supernatural and beyond time. It transcends 'utility' and must not be reduced to a 'thing;' *it must never be 'used.'*

Karol Wojtyla (Pope John Paul II) points out in his anthropological study, *Person and Community,* that the person "finds its natural complement in freedom."[354] The soul of the human person has an inner dynamic, an active interiority —indeed a *conscience* in communion with God. That conscience, reflecting its spiritual mandate, can direct him to do good and avoid evil and thus must always be defended, nourished, and properly directed.

Wojtyla expands on the notion of the grandeur of the human person:

> "The assertion that the human being is a person has profound theoretical significance—I should mention that despite differences in worldviews, everyone in some way agrees with this assertion. In a sense, it marks out the position proper to the human being in the world. It speaks of the human being's natural greatness. The human being holds a position superior to the whole world of nature and stands above everything else in the visible world. This conviction is rooted in experience ...

> " ... Our distinctiveness and superiority as human beings in relation to other creatures is constantly verified by each

one of us ... It is also verified by the whole of humanity in its ongoing experience: in the experience of history, culture, technology, creativity and production. The effects of human activity in various communities testify to this dignity. A being that continually transforms nature, raising it in some sense to that being's own level, must feel higher than nature — and must be higher than it."[355]

In a paper sent to an international conference in Paris in June 1975, entitled "Subjectivity and the Irreducible in the Human Being," Wojtyla writes of the "specialness" and transcendence of each human person and therefore the imperative need to respect its freedom.

"As the need increases to understand the human being as a unique and unrepeatable person ... in other words, as the need increases to understand the personal *subjectivity* of the human being — the category of lived experience takes on greater significance, and, in fact, key significance.

"For then the issue is ... *the revelation of the person as a subject experiencing its acts and inner happenings, and with them its own subjectivity.*"[356]

In lay terms we might say that, uniquely among all other creatures, the human person can live out the divine commands of love of God and of neighbor because it is in a unique relationship to itself, and to others. That is to say, it has the freedom to determine itself by relating to —indeed by *loving*— values (and especially other *persons*, including the Divine Persons) beyond itself.

Here it is particularly helpful to reflect on Wojtyla's notion of the "acting person." Because it is through a person's self-determined actions, —which demand a respect for his freedom, —that he develops himself and his interiority, his special 'personality.'

As he says,

> "My lived experience discloses not only my actions, but also my inner happenings in their profoundest dependence on my own self. It also discloses my whole personal structure of self-determination in which I discover myself as that through which I possess myself and govern myself— or, at any rate, *should* possess myself and govern myself."[357]

Thus, freedom of conscience, brought to fruition by love and so richly defended by our Founders, is critical to authentic human development. Because, as Wojtyla points out:

> "Our decisions of conscience at each step reveal us as persons who fulfill ourselves by going beyond ourselves toward values accepted in truth and realized, therefore, with a deep sense of responsibility."[358]

Given the self-determining capacities of the human person, Wojtyla then addresses the question of morality, i.e., a person's freedom to choose according to the true and the good (or not). He writes:

> "Experience teaches that the *morale* is very deeply rooted in the *humanum*, or, more precisely, in what should be defined as the *personale.*
>
> "Morality defines the personalistic dimension of the human being in a fundamental way; it is subjectified in this dimension and can also be properly understood only in it. At the same time, however, the *morale* is a basic expression of the transcendence proper to the personal self."[359]

These higher faculties of the human person —reason and free will—are not 'things' and obviously transcend materiality and individuality. They "express and actualize" the soul's spirituality—that *divine thing* — and are also "the principal means, so to speak, whereby the human person is actualized; based on their activity, the whole psychological and moral personality takes shape."

And, addressing the *theocentric* dynamic of human personality— a dynamic not only understood but embraced by the Founders— he continues:

> "The dignity of the human person finds its full confirmation in the very fact of revelation, for this fact signifies the establishment of contact between God and the human being. To the human being, created in 'the image and likeness of God,' God communicates God's own thoughts and plans. But this is not all. God also *becomes a human being.* God enters into the drama of human existence and permeates the human being with divine grace.
>
> "For those of us who are believers, this is where the dignity of the human person finds its fullest confirmation; this is where it is, so to speak, brought to the surface. Religion, as Paul VI points out, is a dialogue: through religion God confirms the personal dignity of the human being. The believer finds this confirmation in religion. This may be described as a confirmation 'from above.'"[360]

The Heart of Democracy: The Human Person

It is at the heart of democracy to protect the basic good of collective and individual life: the dignity of the human person. This human person is at once a member of the body politic and a child of God, and is not only capable of serving —but is also *obligated*— to serve both. He is at once a citizen of both worlds; the depth of his faith will only be an enhancement of his ability to serve his fellow men.

Maritain, good Thomist that he is, holds that the human person is, in fact, the fundamental subject of *all* social and political philosophy and is, therefore, at the very core of authentic democracy. He advances this conviction with the greatest emphasis, to the point of holding that if we want to "save civilization," the (false and incomplete) "humanism of the individual and the democracy of the individual, upon which the nineteenth century placed its hopes, must be replaced today by humanism of the person and by democracy of the person."[361]

We could fairly say that all of the social evils of modern times, from slavery to socialism to bourgeois capitalism, have their roots in a false "humanism of the individual," typically resulting in a selfish utilitarianism that diminishes, degrades and, all too often, destroys the human person. We witness this today, so very tragically, in widespread abortion. Not to recognize the uniqueness and *quid divinum* of the human person —and the reality that the person, *qua person*, transcends the collection of individuals that constitute community— is certainly one of modernity's gravest evils.

The Individual

Maritain's notion of the individual derives from a classical distinction between individuality and personality that is fundamental to the doctrine of Aquinas and to the social teachings of the Catholic Church. As distinct from "person," the notion of "individual" operates on a horizontal (non-interior and non-reflective) dimension only, and, therefore, should be thought of as one among many rather than unique and self-determining.

According to Aquinas, the notion of individuality, of both inanimate and animate things, is rooted in matter and in location in space. For the human being, as for all other corporeal beings, individuality has its roots in the singular and the material. It is the realm of the 'what' rather than the 'who.'

In each of us, individuality is that which differentiates us, physically and spatially, from all others. In-so-far as we are individuals, we are one among many, a mere dot in the immense network of forces and influences— cosmic, ethnic, historic— whose forces we obey. As individuals, we are subject to the laws and determination of the physical world.[362]

But what about the roots of modern individualism —the false 'exaltation of the self' which seems to so characterize our age? Maritain would say it was born, or at least profoundly nourished by, the subjectivism of Rousseau and Descartes and the subjective turn of the Enlightenment. By a turning of the subject *from itself* —grounded in the obligations of the two great commandments —to a turning of the subject, first and foremost, *toward itself.* By reducing the inner, dialogic character of the person, to monologue.

All of which was greatly abetted, in the religious realm, by Martin Luther's revolutionary break with tradition, with his defense of egocentrism and with his unbridled projection of self —an individualistic *pretense* of personality —into the world of eternal truths. As Cardinal Ratzinger has written, "Luther's insistence on 'by faith alone' clearly and exactly excludes love from the question of salvation. Love belongs to the realm of 'works' and, thus becomes, 'profane'." [363]

Luther's self "was in his opinion the center round which all humanity should gravitate; he made himself the universal man in whom all should find their model. Let us make no bones about it, he put himself in the place of Jesus Christ."[364]

Per Maritain, doctrine comes as an extra for Luther; what counts with him is his life, his history. Thus, Lutheranism is more of a break with the Church and an overflow of Luther's individuality rather than a well-reasoned theological system. If one is looking for a translation of egocentrism into dogma, it can be found in some of the most-noticeable characteristics of his theology. "I do not admit," he writes in June 1522, "that my doctrine can be judged by anyone, even by the angels. He who does not receive my doctrine cannot be saved."[365]

Luther's absorbing concern with the doctrine of salvation is perhaps the best example, demonstrating that the human self—a mystical egocentrism — has become the chief preoccupation of his theology. Luther makes the science of divine things revolve, not around charity and love of God, but around human corruption. And yet, there is the lingering self-doubt: "Were it not that I am a doctor," he once wrote, "the devil would often have slain me with this argument: You have no authority!"[366]

Chapter Sixteen: Democracy and Christian Personalism

"The person is a good towards which the only proper and adequate attitude is love." St. John Paul II

The question becomes, at some point, how this nation preserves its noble direction and protects its precious freedoms—including, first and foremost, that of conscience— and does not succumb to the "isms" of the day: relativism, secularism, materialism, indifferentism, individualism, et al.

And it must be said, first of all, that this preservation is not something strictly or exclusively a legal preservation, however important. Tocqueville, for example, had high praise for the U.S. Constitution. But he also repeatedly insisted that the success of the American democratic experiment was due less to laws created by the people than to the culture they create for themselves. Their "mores" — the widely shared beliefs and habits that constitute the "true and invisible constitution of the republic."[367] What we might call the "vertical, religious and Christian dimensions" of life, inspiring and vivifying the horizontal; the social, political and cultural orders.

Precisely because freedom of conscience is at stake—that spiritual component of life that creates and extends culture — of great concern today should be the preservation and extension of a public conscience and a public culture that embraces the vertical aspects of life, including its religious values. Such that they are not only *not absent* in the public square, but in important ways —from a higher firmament of truth and goodness —are found there in abundance to protect, enlighten and grace our political and social concerns.

Immanuel Kant contributed significantly to the personalist understanding of human dignity. Unlike Hobbes, for whom "the worth of a man" is "his price," and dignity is "the public worth of a man," Kant regarded dignity as "intrinsic worth," i.e., as an absolute value. He posited a dichotomy between price and dignity, whereby "something that has a price can be exchanged for something else of equal value; whereas that which exceeds all price and therefore admits of no equivalent, has a dignity."

Kant's celebrated practical categorical imperative—"Act so as to treat humanity, whether in your own person or in that of another, always as an end and never as a means only"—was incorporated nearly verbatim into Karol Wojtyła's "personalist principle." Wojtyla makes an important clarification of this principle in his *Love and Responsibility*, wherein he distinguishes the absolute dignity or worth of the human person—meaning the person *can never be used*—from virtually the rest of creation, which is meant *precisely* for man's use.[368]

Of note here is that the human person, as 'person' as well as 'individual', is a member of the body politic, and deserves that the absolute dignity that is his—his vertical/theocentric values— be respected.

Respected because the human person, standing at the center of this vertical orientation towards God, is called to a vocation incorporating both this axis of life and that of the horizontal as well, and with a responsibility unique to him. Namely the capacity to love—to freely, selflessly and expansively *give oneself.* Unless this uniqueness is recognized, there is insufficient rationale for pursuing a coherent, viable future.

Whereas individualism seeks the self above all and views others as means to one's own profit or pleasure, personalism seeks to make of the self a gift to another. "Thus," French philosopher Emmanuel Mounier wrote, "if the first condition of individualism is the centralization of the individual in himself, the first condition of personalism is his decentralization, in order to set him in the open perspectives of personal life." [369]

Where individualism hopes to find personal realization in self-interest, personalism asserts the absolute need for openness to others, even as a condition for one's own realization. Wojtyla characterized the two extremes of individualism and collectivism in the following way:

> "On the one hand, persons may easily place their own individual good above the common good of the collectivity, attempting to subordinate the collectivity to themselves and use it for their individual good. This is the error of individualism, which gave rise to liberalism in modern history and to capitalism in economics.

> "On the other hand, society, in aiming at the alleged good of the whole, may attempt to subordinate persons to itself in such a way that the true good of persons is excluded and they themselves fall prey to the collectivity. This is

the error of totalitarianism, which in modern times has borne the worst possible fruit."[370]

The distinctively Christian personalism developed in the twentieth century by Jacques Maritain and others was greatly enriched by Wojtyla in his work mentioned earlier, *Love and Responsibility*, first published in 1960. There he proposed what he termed "the personalistic norm." "This norm, in its negative aspect, states that the person is the kind of good which does not admit of use and *cannot be treated as an object of use* and means to an end. In its positive form the personalistic norm confirms this: the person is a good towards which the only proper and adequate attitude is love."[371]

This is a first principle of Christian personalism: Persons are not to be used but respected, and more importantly, *loved.* In *Gaudium et Spes*, the Second Vatican Council formulated what has come to be considered the key expression of this personalism: "man ... cannot fully find himself except through a sincere gift of himself."[372]

This formula for self-fulfillment offers a key for overcoming the dichotomy frequently felt between personal "realization" and the needs or demands of social life. Personalism also implies inter-personalism, as Benedict XVI stresses in *Caritas in Veritate:* "As a spiritual being, the human creature is defined through interpersonal relations. The more authentically he or she lives these relations, the more his or her own personal identity matures. It is not by isolation that man establishes his worth, but by placing himself in relation with others and with God."[373]

This, again, is not to opt for a "denominationally Christian nation," which our Founders did not intend nor which this book is suggesting. By the mid-1770s, with the multiplicity of Christian sects, they were uniformly behind separation of Church and state. It is to opt for a nation that is "Christian by inspiration," which is precisely what our earliest settlers did intend, which we are suggesting here, and which the Founders had no problem with.

Cultural Renewal, Personal Renewal

There is an intimate but often unrecognized link between personal and cultural renewal. In Dawson's words, "the development of Christian culture and the progress of Christianity in the individual soul are in many ways parallel."[374] Which is a wonderful echo of St. Augustine: "change human beings and the times will change."[375]

Nor should we be discouraged at the recovery task ahead, for as another great Father of the Church, St. John Chrysostom put it: *"The leaven, no matter how small it is, transforms a great mass of flour; so also will you convert the whole world."*[376]

Pope John XXIII, in his great encyclical *Pacem in Terris* (On Establishing Universal Peace in Truth, Justice, Charity, and Liberty), reminded all men that "human society must primarily be considered something pertaining to the spiritual." [377] To freedom, yes, but as importantly to truth, to justice, and to charity. Which is a vital reminder, in modern times, that despite its immersion in "goods and services," the vital and creative power behind every culture is a spiritual one. Only as the richly Christian elements of beauty, of truth, of joy and of goodness recover their natural positions at the center of culture, can they become the guiding lights and mainsprings of all social activity.

We are witnessing today a gradual restructuring of American culture. And whatever the positives of its trajectory, this is often being done— not according to ideals of Christianity —but to those of utility, productivity, expediency, pleasure and personal autonomy. It is a culture seemingly closed to the supernatural and to grace and to the belief that "in God we trust." A culture—a society— where moral issues are often submerged in a river of preoccupations, and where unrelenting economic focus, political 'will to power' and media/celebrity hegemony too often subvert rather than ennoble public life.

Christopher Dawson puts it this way, "Every culture is like a plant. It must have its roots in the earth, and for sunlight it must needs be open to the spiritual. At the present moment we are busy cutting its roots and shutting out all light from above."[378] Christian women and men are called to respond to this cultural challenge. In the words of John Paul II, "We must build a Christian culture ready to evangelize the larger culture in which we live."[379]

This is not to call for a national religion in America, or anywhere else. It is to call for a sincere conscience and a religious attitude that asks people of all faiths in the Almighty to take their faith commitments more seriously. Not, of course, primarily for the concern of the nation— theirs' should be a fundamentally personal, "I-Thou" relationship with God. But realizing, at a deep level, that living this commitment generously is the best thing they can do for their country as well.

This is not a new concept for the United States. The belief that the state, described by the Old Testament metaphor as "nursing fathers," should be supportive of religion had existed for centuries in Western Europe. It was deeply rooted, as historian James Hutson points out, in the mentality and traditions of Anglicans, Congregationalists and Presbyterians.[380]

A former president of Yale, for example, Elisha Williams (1694-1755), claimed that "the Civil Authority of a State are obliged to take

Care for the Support of religion." Religion was felt to be the "great cement of civil society," and should be nourished because a high level of rectitude was needed for the successful establishment of a republican government. "Republican government was, above all, self-government and self-government placed higher demands on the average citizen than any other polity."[381]

A nation of believers is a nation solidified at a spiritual level, with due respect for religious freedom, and also a more virtuous people, better able to manage their personal as well as their community affairs. And thus, says Maritain, "we also understand why civilizations, themselves belonging to the natural order, cannot arrive at their full state and dignity as civilizations, except in so far as they are elevated in their own order by the influence of those virtues which arise in them, not from what is Caesar's but from what is God's."[382]

As Dawson has noted, Christian civilization was a great ferment of social and intellectual change for centuries. It was so precisely because taking responsibility for the world and changing it for the better was an integral part of the Christian cultural ideal. It presented a reality beyond the finite and temporal and provided a force that was culturally creative and transforming.

While Dawson speaks of this creative spiritual force as a thing of the past, he points squarely to the challenge facing Christians today. That is, to reawaken among themselves a deep love and concern for all earthly realities and that "missionary character" —the work of transmitting a spiritual energy from one people to another[383] — such that "the world might be fashioned anew according to God's design and reach its fulfillment."[384]

Dawson clearly saw the limitations of ideology —of "isms"— to authentic cultural change. Ideology, as he points out, is a work of man. It typically presents a false absolutism bound to a political will wanting to shape the culture to its purpose. Lacking a religious foundation and perspective, it lacks the capability to properly shape culture because it fails to understand the deeper realities of the "inner man" — especially creativity and freedom — and is therefore incapable of truly forming that man ... that *person*.

Faith, on the other hand:

> "Looks beyond the world of man and his works; it introduces man to a higher and more universal range of reality than the finite and temporal world to which the state and economic order belong. And thereby it introduces into human life an element of spiritual freedom which may have a creative and transforming influence on man's social culture and historical destiny as well as on his inner personal experience. If therefore we study culture as a whole, we shall find there an intimate relation between its religious faith and its social achievement."[385]

As for the leaders of a renewed Christian civilization we might add here a teaching of Aquinas, namely that whoever has the care of the common well-being of the multitude must be a *bonus vir* (a good man), pure and simple, a virtuous man in every respect.

Would that the Obama administration —and indeed all in government and the body politic— pay serious heed to our unique religious and philosophical traditions, to our Founders' intentions, and to the reflections of our greatest men. They serve not just the common good of Christians. They serve all men and women who can distinguish the things that are Caesar's— and those that are God's. They serve all who wish to freely practice their faith under the protection of their God *and* of their government.

> *Then conquer we must, for our cause it is just—*
> *And this be our motto, "in God is our trust!*[386]

Index

References

1 Abraham Lincoln's First Inaugural, March 4, 1861.

2 Collected Works, VIII, *Lincoln,* 542-543.

3 Matthew 5:14.

4 Martin Luther King Jr., "Letter from a Birmingham Jail," April 16, 1963.

5 Thomas Jefferson, "Letters to the Methodist Episcopal Church at New London," Connecticut, February 4, 1809.

6 Alexis de Tocqueville, *Democracy in America,* 1835 (2004), Lxvii.3, p. 358.

7 Andre Jardin, *Tocqueville: A Biography* (trans. London, 1988).

8 Tocqueville, *Democracy in America,* 1835, (2004) II.i.3, 525.

9 Marcello Pera, *Why We Should Call Ourselves Christians,* 2011, American Edition, footnote p. 183, ref. Hegel 2008, #62n, p17.

10 http://xroads.virginia.edu/~Hyper/DETOC/ch1_03.htm.

11 www.heritage.org/research/.../2004/.../balancing-conscience-and-the-law.

12 caselaw.lp.findlaw.com/scripts/getcase.pl?navby=CASE&court..

13 Peter Drucker, "Organized Religion and the American Creed," *The Review of Politics,* p. 299–300, July, 1956

14 CP Blogs, July 9, 2010.

15 www.allabouthistorh.org/year-of-the-bible-htm

16 www.govtrack.us/congress/bills/111hconres121text.

17 Steven Prothero, *Wall Street Journal,* A13, Jan. 18, 2013.

18 Mary Pipher, *The Shelter of Each Other,* Ballantine, 1996, p. 81.

[19] Inaugural Addresses of the Presidents of the United States from George Washington 1789 to Harry S. Truman 1949, 82nd Congress, 2nd Session, House Document No. 540, 1952.

[20] Cardinal Ratzinger interview with newspaper *La Repubblica* on November 19, 2004.

[21] Kay Brigham, *Christopher Columbus: His Life and Discovery in the Light of His Prophecies*, Libros CLIE, 1990,

[22] E. Gaustad and L. Schmidt, *The Religious History of America*, Harper One, 2002, p. 16.

[23] Ibid, p. 16.

[24] en.wikiquote.org/wiki/Christopher_Columbus

[25] op.cit.. Brigham, 1990, p. 31.

[26] op.cit.. Brigham, 1990, p. 62.

[27] op.cit.. Gaustad and Schmidt, p.16.

[28] Ibid, p. 17.

[29] William Warren Sweet, *The Story of Religion in America*, Harper & Brothers, N.Y. 1950, p. 9.

[30] en.wikipedia.org/wiki/Jamestown-Settlers.

[31] en.wikipedia.org/wiki/Robert_Hunt_(chaplain)

[32] William Bradford, *On Plymouth Plantation*.

[33] William Warren Sweet, *Religion in Colonial America*, Cooper Square Publishers, New York, 1965, p. 327.

[34] op.cit.. Gaustad and Schmidt, p. 67.

[35] www.scribd.com/.../The-New-England-Mind-From-Colony-to-Province.

[36] Perry Miller, *The New England Mind, The Seventeenth Century*, The Belknap Press of Harvard University Press,1982, p. 4.

[37] Ibid, p. 4.

[38] Ibid, p. 107.

[39] Ibid, p. 22.

[40] Ibid, p. 4-5.

[41] Philip Schaff, *History of the Christian Church*, Vol. 3, C. Scribner's Son, 1908, p. 997.

[42] www.newadvent.org/cathen/02091a.htm.

[43] Adolph Harnack. *The Essence of Christianity*, Fourteenth Lesson; www.newadvent.org › Catholic Encyclopedia

[44] Adolph Harnack, *History of Dogma* (English translation, V,234-235).

[45] Gibbon, *Decline and Fall*, Ch. 23, note in Harper's ed., Vol 3, p. 271.

[46] Pope Leo XIII, Encyclical *Immortale Dei*, Nov. 1, 1885.

[47] St. Augustine, *Confessions,* trans. By Frank Sheed, Hackett Publishing Company, Inc. 1993, p. 38.

[48] John H. Taylor, S.J., "St. Augustine and the Hortensius of Cicero," *Studies in Philology*, July, 1963.

[49] op.cit.. St. Augustine, *Confessions,* p. 38-39.

[50] Thomas Jefferson, "Letter to Henry Lee," 8 May, 1825, in *The Political Thought of American Statesmen*, eds. Morton Frisch and Richard Stevens, F.E. Peacock Publishers, 1973, p.12.

[51] James S. Reid, "Academica of Cicero," The Text Revised and Explained, Cicero Collections, Christ's College, Cambridge, December, 1873. See also: www.bartleby.com › ... › Harvard Classics › Cicero › On Friendship

[52] Pope Gelasius I, "Letter to the Emperor Anastasius on Spiritual and Temporal Power," trans. In J.H. Robinson, *Readings in European History*, Boston: Ginn, 1905, p. 72-73.

[53] *Catechism of the Catholic Church*, No. 2003.

[54] *Catechism of the Catholic Church*, No. 2001.

[55] *Catechism of the Catholic Church*, No. 2002.

[56] Genesis 1:27-28; Matthew 5: 48.

[57] James I. Packer and O.R. Johnson, *Introduction to Martin Luther's Bondage of the Will*, p. 273, p. 103-104, and p. 204.

[58] Ibid, p. 58.

[59] Ibid, p. 217.

[60] Jacques Maritain, *True Humanism*, Greenwood Press, 1941, reprinted 1970, p.9.

[61] Louis Bouyer, *The Spirit and Forms of Protestantism*, Scepter Publishers, Princeton, New Jersey, 2001, p.16. Ibid, p. 17.

[62] Ibid,. p.16.

[63] Ibid,. p. 16-17.

[64] Ibid,. p. 17.

[65] St.Thomas Aquinas, *Summa Theologica*, I, II, 82-83

[66] *Catechism of the Catholic Church*, 1996, (Cf. Jn.1:12-18, Rom.14-17, 2 Pet: 13-14).

[67] St. Augustine, In Jo.Ev 72,3:PL 35,1823).

[68] www.vatican.va/archive/ccc_css/archive/catechism/p3s1c3a2.htm

[69] Jacques Maritain, *The Degrees of Knowledge*, University of Notre Dame Press, 2002, p.322.

[70] Ibid, p. 323.

[71] Ibid, p. 323.

[72] *CCC* 2002.

[73] St. Augustine, *Confessions* 13,3, 51:PL 32, 868; Genesis 131

[74] St. Thomas Aquinas, *Summa Theologica* II, II, 5, 3.

[75] John Calvin, *Institution II*, v. 19.

[76] Gretillat, "Dogmatique" III. Stevens, Bruce and Mozley, on the Augustinian Doctrine of Predestination.

[77] Maritain, www.nd.edu/Departments/Maritain/etext/augustin.htm.

[78] Jacques Maritain, *True Humanism*, Greenwood Press, 1941, p. 12-13.

[79] Boettner, *Reformed Doctrine of Predestination*, 382.

[80] S.J. Han, An Investigation into Calvin's use of Augustine ... see website.

[81] newadvent.org/cathen/02091a.htm

[82] en.wikipedia.org/wiki/Jansenism

[83] St. Augustine, www.ewtn.com/library/.../TA-CAT.t...

[84] Perry Miller, *The New England Mind: The Seventeenth Century*, The Belknap Press of Harvard University Press, p. 104.

[85] Ibid, p. 104.

[86] Ibid, p. 94.

[87] Perry Miller, *Orthodoxy in Massachusetts*, Cambridge, 1933 xi.

[88] Murray G. Murphy, "Perry Miller and American Studies," *American Studies*, 42:2, Summer 2001, 5-18.

[89] Book jacket quotes from Niebuhr and Hoopes, from *The New England Mind*. Also quote from Mark Noll, author of *A History of Christianity in the United States and Canada*, see prev. reference.

[90] http://en.wikipedia.org/wiki/St._Augustine,_Florida.

[91] http://en.wikipedia.org/wiki/Jun%C3%ADpero_Serra.

[92] John Eidsmoe, *Christianity and the Constitution*, Baker Books, 1987, p. 19.

[93] Mark Noll, *A History of Christianity in the United States and Canada*, Eerdmans Publishing Co., 1992, reprinted 2003, p. 14.

[94] William Warren Sweet, *The Story of Religion in America,* Harper & Brothers, N.Y., 1950, p. 184.

[95] Churchvstate.blogspot.com2009/08Charles-carroll-founding father.

[96] Paul Johnson, *History of the American People*, Harper Collins, 1997, p.110.

[97] Ibid, p. 109.

[98] Wikipedia.org/wiki/First_Great_Awakening.

[99] Ibid.

[100] op.cit.. Paul Johnson, 1997, p.111.

[101] St. Thomas Aquinas, *Summa Theologica*, I-II, 110.2. ad.2.

[102] Ibid, *Summa Theologica*, I-II,110.2. ad 3.

[103] op.cit.. Johnson, 1997, p. 112.

[104] *Norman Fiering, "Will and Intellect* in the New England Mind," *William and Mary Quarterly*, 3d ser., 29 (1972): 519-20.

[105] See idem, "Solomon Stoddard's Library at Harvard," Harvard Library Bulletin 20 (1972), 262-269.

[106] op.cit... Mark Noll, A History of Christianity in the United States and Canada, 1992, p. 87.

[107] Anri Morimoto, *Jonathan Edwards and the Catholic Vision of Salvation*, The Pennsylvania State University, 1995, p. 41-42.

[108] Virtueonline News Theology Research...Jonathan Edwards on Justification by Faith

[109] op.cit.. Morimoto, *Jonathan Edwards*, p. 52-53.

[110] op.cit.. Paul Johnson, *History of the American People*, p. 12.

[111] Wikipedia.org/wiki/First_Great_Awakening

[112] op cit. Mark Noll, *A History of Christianity*, p. 91.

[113] George Whitefield, *Works,* Vol. I, Letter CCCCLVIII, 486,487, September 24, 1742, 486-487.

[114] Cfr. http://www.mwrc.ac.uk/whitefield-conference/

[115] en.wikipedia.org/wiki/John_Witherspoon

[116] Garry Wills, *Explaining America: The Middle and Southern States, 1783-1837,* University of Alabama Press, 1980, p. 2.

[117] Thomas Miller, ed. *The Selected Writings of John Witherspoon,* Carbondale, Il. Southern Illinois University Press, 1990, p. 137-138.

[118] Ibid. p. 140-141.

[119] William Warren Sweet, *Religion in the Development of American Culture, 1765-1840,* New York, Scribner 1952, p.8.

[120] op.cit... Miller, *Selected Writings,* 1990, p. 144.

[121] books.google.com/books?isbn+1444393626, St. Augustine, *City of God.,*

[122] John Witherspoon, "Sermon on the Dominion of Providence," p. 93, quoted by Hosmer, "Of Divine Providence," p. 15.

[123] John Ramsey Witherspoon, quoted by Stohlman, John Witherspoon, p. 173.

[124] John Eidsmoe, *Christianity and the Constitution,* Baker Books, 1987, p. 92.

[125] Ibid, William Warren Sweet, *The Story of Religion in America,* Harper Brothers, 1950, p. 224.

[126] Ibid. p. 226.

[127] Donald S. Lutz, "The Relative Influence of European Writers on Late Eighteenth Century American Political Thought," *American Political Science Review* (1984), p. 189-197.

[128] justus.anglican.org/resources/bio/64.html

[129] Richard Hooker, *Of the Laws of Ecclesiastical Polity,* V.53.3.

[130] Newworldencyclopedis.org/entry/Richard-Hooker

[131] op cit. Richard Hooker, *Laws,* viii, 4.

[132] books.google.com/books?isbn=1579102131

[133] Christopher Dawson, *The Crisis of Western Education,* Sheed and Ward, 1961, p. 37.

[134] John Witte, Jr., quoted in P. Hamburger, *Separation of Church and State,* 2002, p. 23. Footnote.

[135] Ibid, Hamburger, p. 22.

[136] op.cit.. Richard Hooker, *Of the Laws of Ecclesiastical Polity,* 1.12.2.

[137] Ibid, 1.11.4.

[138] Ibid,1.14.1.

[139] Alex.P. D'Entreves, *The Medieval Contributions to Political Thought*, The Humanities Press, N.Y. 1959, p. 118.

[140] William E. Gladstone, *The State in its Relation with the Church*, J. Murray, London, 1841, p. 14.

[141] op.cit... A.P D'Entreves, p. 142.

[142] http://en.wikipedia.org/wiki/Richard_Hooker

[143] http://en.wikipedia.org/wiki/Richard_Hooker, John Locke, *Second Treatise on Civil Government*, Chapter 11.

[144] John Locke, *Two Treatises of Government*, London, A. Bettesworth, 1728 Book II, p. 234, Ch. XI, #135, p. 234.

[145] www.wallbuilders.com/libissuesarticles.asp?id=99156

[146] "Of the General Principles of Law and Obligation", Bird Wilson, editor. Philadelphia: Lorenzo Press, 1804, Vol. I, pp 66-68.

[147] www.wallbuilders.com/libissuesarticles.asp?-id991565

[148] John Quincy Adams, *The Jubilee of the Constitution: A Discourse Delivered at the Request of the York Historical Society, etc.* New York: Samuel Colman, 1839, p. 40.

[149] www.wallbuilders, Issue and Articles, John Locke, *A Philosophical Founder of America*, Id 99156

[150] Ibid

[151] Ibid

[152] Ibid

[153] Ibid

[154] Ibid

[155] James Wilson, *On the General Principles of Law and Obligation*, Lii.2266.

[156] James Madison, "Examination of the British Doctrine," 1806, quoted by Hall, *Christian History of the Constitution*, p. 250.

[157] Jefferson, Letter to Henry Lee, May 8, 1825.

[158] Adams and Novangelus, No. 1.

[159] John Adams: *Defence of the Constitutions: Vol. I, Letter XXVI.*

[160] Montesquieu, *The Spirit of the Laws*, Volume II, 28, 29.

[161] books.google.com/books?id=3yEUAAAAYAAJ

162 www.newadvent.org/cathen/10536a.htm.

163 books.google.com/books?isbn=0897748522

164 John Henry Cardinal Newman, *Certain Difficulties Felt by Anglicans in Catholic Teaching II*, Long, Longmans Green, 1885, p. 248.

165 Vatican II, *Gaudium et Spes*, 16.

166 St. Augustine, In ep.Jo.8,9: PL 35, 2041.

167 op.cit. *Gaudium et Spes*, 16.

168 Karol Wojtyla, *Person and Community: Selected Essays*, Peter Lang Publishers, 2008, 190.

169 op.cit... *Gaudium et Spes*, chapter one on "The Dignity of the Human Person."

170 John Locke, *Introduction to the Second Treatise of Government*, ed. Thomas P. Peardon, Indianapolis, Bobbs-Merrill, Library of Liberal Art, 1952.

171 Carl L. Becker, four lectures on The Enlightenment, Yale University, "The Heavenly City of the Eighteenth-Century Philosophers,"1932.

172 Ritchie, Natural Rights, p. 39, from Carl Becker, *The Declaration of Independence*, Vintage Book, p. 38.

173 173.Sophocles, Antigone 452-60, from Jacques Maritain, *Man and the State*, University of Chicago Press 1951, p. 85.

174 St. Thomas Aquinas, *Summa Theologica*, I-IIae., q. 91, art. 2.

175 Etienne Gilson, *The Christian Philosophy of Saint Augustine*, Vintage, 1967, p. 130-131.

176 John Courtney Murray, S.J., *We Hold These Truths: Catholic Reflections on the American Proposition*, Sheed and Ward, 1960, p. 40.

177 Ibid, p. 300.

178 Ibid, p. 28.

179 Ibid, p. 29.

180 Ibid, p. 29

181 Russell Kirk, "The Dissolution of Liberalism," *Commonweal*, January 7, 1955.

182 op.cit.. Marcello Pera, *Why We Should Call Ourselves Christians*, p. 114, refer. Kant 1996, d.118 (7:90-91).

183 Immanuel Kant, *Groundwork of the Metaphysics of Morals* (1785), trans. H.J. Paton, New York, Harper & Row, 1964, p. 75.

184 Immanuel Kant, *Critique of Practical Reason*, 1788, trans. Lewis White Beck, Indianapolis: Bobbs Merrill, 1956, p. 18.

[185] Friedrich Paulsen, *Immanuel Kant*, New York, Scribners's Sons, 1902, p. 11.

[186] www3.nd.edu/Departments/.../perrier0.University of Notre Dame

[187] Immanuel Kant 1997, AK 2K 27:372, p. 147.

[188] John Locke 1988, #. 6, pp. 270-71, from Pera footnotes p. 188-189.

[189] op.cit. Marcello Pera, , footnote #78.

[190] Jacques Maritain, *Christianity and Democracy*, Ignatius Press, 1986, 28-29.

[191] James Hutson, *Religion and the Founding of the American Republic*, University Press of New England, 1998, p. 49.

[192] Ibid, p. 49.

[193] Ibid, p. 49.

[194] Ibid, p. 49.

[195] Ibid, p. 50.

[196] Frank Monaghan, *John Jay, Defender of Liberty,* Indianapolis: Bobbs Merrill, reprinted 1972, p. ix, quoting Richard Hildreth, 19th century Federalist historian.

[197] John Eidsmoe, *Christianity and the Constitution*, Baker Books, 1987, p. 166.

[198] John Jay, *Address to New York Convention*, December 23, 1776, Ibid, I: p.55.

[199] Ibid, I: p.56.

[200] Ibid, I: p.50.

[201] Norman Cousins, *In God We Trust*, quoting John Jay to Jedidiah Morse, January 1, 1813. Harper & Brothers, 1958, p. 363-364.

[202] op.cit. Hutson, p. 52.

[203] Ibid, p. 52.

[204] Ibid, p. 52.

[205] Ibid, p. 53.

[206] William Warren Sweet, *The Story of Religion in America*, Harper, 1950, www.theamericanconservative.com/.../wa..

[207] William Warren Sweet, *The Story of Religion in America*, Harper, 1950, p. 173.

[208] Samuel Williams, *The Influence of Christianity on Civil Society*, Boston, 1780, 20-21.

[209] James Hutson, *Religion and the Founding of the American Republic,* Library of Congress, 1998, Washington, p. 56-57.

[210] Paul Johnson, *The Founding Father, George Washington*, Harper Collins Books, 2005, p. 102-103.

[211] Anson Phelps Stokes, *Church and State in the United States,* 1950, p. 515.

[212] Norman Cousins, *In God We Trust, Harper,* 1958, p.51.

[213] op.cit. P. Johnson, 2005, p. 103.

[214] http://en.wikipedia.org/wiki/George_Washington's_Farewell_Address

[215] www.loc.gov/exhibits/religion/rel 196.html

[216] Eric Rosenberg, "The Whispers of Democracy in Ancient Judaism," *Wall Street Journal,* Sept. 21, 2012, A13.

[217] Edmund Burke, *The Speeches of the Right Hon. Edmund Burke,* with Memoir and Historical Introduction by James Burke, Esq. A.B., Dublin, James Duffy and Co., Ltd. 1858, p.445.

[218] James Madison quoted in the introduction to *The Federalist Papers* by Alexander Hamilton, James Madison and John Jay, ed. Garry Will. Toronto: Bantam Books, 1982, p. xxi.

[219] James Madison, *Federalist 51,* p. 261.

[220] Russell Kirk, *The Wise Men Know Wicked Things are Written on the Sky,* Washington, D.C., Regnery Gateway, Inc., 1987, p. 110.

[221] John Adams quoted in John Eidsmoe, "The Religious Roots of the Constitution," *The New Federalist Papers,* ed. J. Jackson Barlow, Dennis J. Mahoney and John G. West Jr., Lanham; University Press of America, 1988, p. 274.

[222] http://en.wikipedia.org/wiki/Second_Great_Awakening

[223] William Warren Sweet, *The Story of Religion in America,* Harper & Brothers, New York. 1950, p. 233.

[224] Ibid, p. 224.

[225] Ibid, p. 223.

[226] Ibid, p. 224.

[227] op cit., Paul Johnson, *A History of the American People,* p. 297.

[228] Edwin Gaustad and Leigh Schmidt, *The Religious History of America,* Harper One, 2004, p. 139.

[229] Ibid, p.139.

[230] Ibid, p.139.

[231] op.cit.. Paul Johnson, p. 297.

[232] Ibid, Paul Johnson, p. 297.

[233] Ibid, Paul Johnson, p. 297.

[234] op.cit.. Gaustad and Schmidt, *The Religious History of America*, Harper One, 2004. p. 145.

[235] Ibid, Gaustad & Schmidt, p. 145.

[236] Wikipedia, *Second Great Awakening*, 5/10.

[237] Timothy S. Smith, *Revivalism and Social Reform: American Protestantism on the Eve of the Civil War*, New York, Abingdon Press, 1957; www.monticello.org/.../jefferson/quotations-jefferson-memori...

[238] op.cit.. Marcello Pera, footnote, p. 6; en.wikiquote.org/wiki/James_Madison

[239] www.freerepublic.com/focus/news/1277493/replies? C=68

[240] George Weigel, *Against the Grain,* The Crossroad Publishing Company, 2008, p. 205, referencing James Madison's *Memorial and Remonstrance.*

[241] John Eidsmoe, *Christianity and the Constitution,* Baker Books, Grand Rapids, 1987, p. 109.

[242] James Madison, "Property," in *The National Gazette,* March 29, 1792.

[243] Richard Brookhiser, *America's First Dynasty: The Adamses,* 1735-1918, The Free Press, p. 13.

[244] *The Works of John Adams* (1854), vol. III, p. 421, diary entry for July 26, 1796.

[245] John Adams to Thomas Jefferson, June 28th, 1813, from Quincy. *The Adams-Jefferson Letters: The Complete Correspondence Between Thomas Jefferson and Abigail and John Adams*, edited by Lester J. Cappon, 1988, the University of North Carolina Press, Chapel Hill, NC, pp. 338-340.

[246] John Adams, *The Works of John Adams,* Charles Francis Adams, editor. Boston: Little Brown and Company, 1856, Vol. X. pp 45-46, to Thomas Jefferson on June 28, 1813.

[247] Fisher Ames, Palladium (January, 1801), wikiquote.

[248] en.wikiquote.org/wiki/John_Quincy_Adams

[249] Ibid, Wikipedia

[250] Rev. Edward J. Gidding, *American Christian Rulers,* New York: Bromfield & Co.,1890, p. 6-13.

[251] Joseph Blunt (1830), *The American Annual Register for the Years 1827 - 8 -9* (New York: E.&G. W. Blunt, 29:300.

[252] op.cit. *American Christian Rulers, or* books.google.com/books?isbn= 0892216298

[253] http://www.adherents.com/gov/Founding_Fathers_Religion.html

[254] B.J. Lossing, *Signers of the Declaration of Independence*, George F. Cooledge & Brothers: New York, reprinted in Lives of the Signers of the Declaration of Independence, WallBuilders Press: Aledo, Texas (1995), p.7-12.

[255] en.wikipedia.org/wiki/United_States_Declaration_of_Independence.

[256] Walter Lippmann, *New York Herald Tribune*, Jan. 7th, 1939.

[257] *Catholic News*, Jan. 17th, 1942.

[258] Vice President Henry Wallace, "The Price of Free World Victory," speech delivered on May 8, 1942, before the Free World Association.

[259] *New York Times*, April 13, 1942.

[260] Harry S. Truman speech, White House Grounds, December 24, 1945.

[261] www.archives.gov/publications/prologue/2009/spring/truman-history.htm. See also *Harry S. Truman, Memoirs,* Doubleday, 1955.

[262] David McCullough, *Truman,* Simon & Schuster, N.Y., 1992, p. 729.

[263] http://millercenter.org/president/speeches/detail/3352

[264] Robert Rhodes (ed), *Winston S. Churchill: His Complete Speeches 1897-1963. Vol. VII:* 1943-1949 (New York: Chelsea House Publishers 1974.

[265] Henri Bergson, *The Two Sources of Morality and Religion*, English Ed., p. 243.

[266] Jacques Maritain, *Man and the State,* University of Chicago Press, 1951, p. 183-184.

[267] Christopher Dawson, *Understanding Europe*, Sheed and Ward, 1952, p.23.

[268] Jacques Maritain, *Christianity and Democracy*, Ignatius Press, 1986 p. 24-25.

[269] Jacques Maritain, *Scholasticism and Politics*, Image Books, 1960, p. 225.

[270] www.traces-cl.com/dic04/thefatherof.html

[271] wikipedia.org/wiki/Jean_Monnet

[272] R.W. Keyserlingk, *Fathers of Europe*, Palm Publishers Limited, Montreal, 1972, p. 139.

[273] ilussidiaro.net/News/English-Culture-Religion-Science-2009/7/15.../31203

[274] op.cit.. Keyserlingk, 1972.

[275] Pope John Paul II Address at European Act in Santiago de Compostela, November 9, 1982.

[276] Ibid, John Paul II.

277 Wikipedia.org/wiki/Religion_in_the_European_Union, also http://www. pinknews.co.uk/news/articles/2005—1863.html; http://europa.eu/about-eu/ countries/member-countries/index_en.htm

278 Paul Belien, "European Parliament Backs Gay Marriage," http://www. Brusselsjournal.com/node/696

279 Marcello Pera, *Why We Should Call Ourselves Christians*: Encounter Books, New York, 2008, p. 128.

280 Michael Pakaluk, "Religion in a Liberal Democracy," *The Naked Public Square Reconsidered*, Chris Wolfe, Ed. ISI Books, 2009, p. 86.

281 George Weigel, "Europe's Problem—and Ours," *First Things,* February, 2004.

282 juicyecumenism.com/.../angela-merkel-christianity-is-the-worlds-most-pe...

283 hollowverse.com/angela-merkel/

284 Philip Jenkins, *God's Continent*, Oxford University Press, 2007, p. 6.

285 www.firstthings.com/article.2007/01/europesquos-problemmdashand-ours-9

286 *Washington Post*, May 14, 2009.

287 Birth Data, http://www.cdc.gov/nchs/nvss.htm: Child Trends (2012) Percentage of Births to Unmarried Women: Retrieved from: www.childtrends-databank.org/?q=node/196. March 2012.

288 . *Wall Street Journal*, March 10-11, 2012.

289 Ibid, *WSJ*

290 http://www.foxnews.com/opinion/2012/05/09/what-obama-must-not-say-about-those-who-dont-support-gay-marriage/#ixzz1uPGUGLMr).

291 www. Chicagotribune.com/news.chi-obama-gay-marriage, 0, 441619.story

292 Hadley Arkes, "Looking Back from 2034," from *The Naked Public Square Reconsidered*. Ed. By Ch. Wolfe, ISI Books, 2009.

293 op cit. Cardinal Ratzinger, *La Repubblica*.

294 Marcello Pera, *Why We Should Call Ourselves Christians*, Encounter Books, 2011, p. 45.

295 Ibid, p. 15-16.

296 Ibid, p. 41.

297 Ibid, p. 16.

[298] nn.us/articles/132813.html

[299] James H. Hutson, *Religion and the Founding of the American Republic*, Library of Congress, Preface, 1998, xii.

[300] Patrick N. Garry, "The Myth of Separation: America's Historical Experience with Church and State," *Hofstra Law Review*, Vol. 33, 475, p. 498.

[301] Ursula Henriques, "Religious Toleration in England: 1787-1833," at 5-6, (1961), *Hofstra Law Review*, p. 482.

[302] Philip Hamburger, *Separation of Church and State*, Harvard U. Press, 2002, p. 162.

[303] www.godvoter.com

[304] op.cit.. Hamburger, 2002, p. 11.

[305] en.wikipedia.org/wiki/Northwest_ordinance.

[306] op.cit.. Johnson, 1997, p.144.

[307] op.cit.. G. Weigel, *Catholicism and the Renewal of American Democracy*, Paulist Press, 1989, p. 18.

[308] Walter Isaacson, *Benjamin Franklin, An American Life*, Simon & Schuster, 2003, p. 94, from Franklin Autobiography 139.

[309] Ibid, p. 110-111.

[310] www.loc.gov/exhibits/religion/rel106.html.

[311] Robert Bellah, *Civil Religion in America*, (need rest of ref.)

[312] www.robertbellah.com/articles_5.htm

[313] press-pubs.uchicago.edu/Founders/documents/a1_8_18s16.html

[314] www.freerepublic.com/focus/f-news/2979170/posts

[315] op.cit.. Hamburger, 2002, p. 451.

[316] Ibid, Hamburger, 2002, p. 426.

[317] Lawrence M. Friedman, *American Law in the 20th Century*, Yale University Press, 2002, p. 510.

[318] op.cit.. Hamburger, 2002, p. 477.

[319] Peter Drucker, "Organized Religion and the American Creed," *The Review of Politics*, p. 301-302, July, 1956.

[320] op.cit.. Friedman, p. 513.

[321] Ibid, Friedman, p. 516.

[322] John Wesley Cooper, *The Theology of Freedom*, Mercer University Press, 1985, p. 93-94.

[323] Jacques Maritain, *Challenges and Renewals*, University of Notre Dame Press, 1966, p. 300.

[324] http://en.wikipedia.org/wiki/Engel_v._Vitale#The_Court.27s_decision

[325] en.wikipedia.org/.../Separation_of_church_and_state_in_the_

[326] op.cit.. Friedman, *American Law*, p. 511.

[327] http://en.wikiquote.org/wiki/William_Rehnquist

[328] http://www.law.cornell.edu/supremecourt/text/512/687, also http://en.wikipedia.org/wiki/Board_of_Education_of_Kiryas_Joel_Village_School_District_v._Grumet.

[329] www.gallup.com/poll/147887/americans-continue-believe-god.aspx.

[330] op.cit.. Patrick M. Garry, "The Myth of Separation: America's Historical Experience with Church and State", *Hofstra Law Review,* Vol. 33, 2004.

[331] morallaw.org/blog/2006/09/the-ten-commandments-in-the-supreme-court-building

[332] Newt Gingrich, *Rediscovering God in America*, Thomas Nelson, 2009, p. 130-131.

[333] *Wall Street Journal*, October 2, 2012, A3.

[334] *Wall Street Journal*, Thursday, May 9, 2013.

[335] Jacques Maritain, *Man and the State*, The University of Chicago Press, 1951, p. 182-183.

[336] Ibid, p. 183-184.

[337] Vatican II, *Gaudium et Spes*, No. 22.

[338] Christopher Dawson, *Enquiries into Religion and Culture*, 1933, p. xvii-xviii.

[339] Christopher Dawson, *Understanding Europe*, Sheed and Ward, 1952, p. 23.

[340] op.cit.. Marcello Pera, p. 115.

[341] Cardinal Ratzinger, *Values in a Time of Upheaval*, St.Ignatius Press, 2006, p. 47.

[342] Ibid, p. 47.

[343] Ibid, p. 47.

[344] Ibid, p. 48.

345 Ibid, p. 49.

346 Letter from Paige Rodriguez, Louisville, Co., to *Wall Street Journal Opinion*, March 14, 2012, A12.

347 Ibid, *WSJ*, March 14, 2012.

348 en.wikipedia.org/.../Religious_affiliation_in_the_United_States

349 Pewforum.org., "Faith on the Hill, The Religious Composition of the 112th Congress," Feb. 28, 2011. (relates to 2 paragraphs, p. 101)

350 Karol Wojtyla, *Person and Community*: Selected Essays, trans. by Theresa Sandok, OSM (New York: Peter Lang, 1993), p. 190.

351 Ibid, Karol Wojtyla, p. 190.

352 John Paul II, Meeting with Young People, Madrid, May 3, 2003

353 Christopher Dawson, *Christianity and the New Age*, Sophia Press, p. 101-102.

354 op cit. Karol Wojtyla, *Person and Community*, Lang, 1993, p. 167.

355 Ibid, Wojtyla, p. 178.

356 Ibid, Wojtyla, address given in Paris, June 13-14, 1975, p. 212.

357 Ibid, Wojtyla, Lang, 1993, p. 214.

358 Ibid, Wojtyla, Lang, p. 214-215.

359 Ibid, Wojtyla, Lang, p. 168.

360 Ibid, Wojtyla, Lang, p. 179-80.

361 Jacques Maritain, *Scholasticism and Politics*, Image, 1960, p. 61.

362 Ibid, Maritain, p. 66.

363 Cardinal Ratzinger interview, "Luther and the Unity of the Churches," *Communio*, International Catholic Review II, 1984.

364 Jacques Maritain, *Three Reformers,* Charles Scribner. New York, 1950, p.15, taken from Johann Adam Möhler (1796-1838), German Catholic priest and theologian.

365 Ibid, Maritain, p. 15, ref. Erl.., 28, 144

366 Walch, Luther's *Werke*, XXII, 1035-1036.

367 op.cit.. Tocqueville, *Democracy in America*, p. 308.

368 en.wikipedia.org/wiki/Categorical_imperativeImmanual Kant.

369 Plato.stanford.edu/entries/personalism

370 books.google.com/books?isbn=081321391

371 *www.catholicculture.com/jp2_on_l&r.pdf* Karol Wojtyla

[372] *Gaudium et Spes*, Vatican II, 24.

[373] *en.wikipedia.org/wiki/Personalism*

[374] *payingattentiontothesky.com/.../christopher-dawson-on-sanctifying-the-p...*

[375] www9.georgetown.edu/faculty/jod/twayne/aug3.html 9 check orig. St. A. source

[376] St. John Chrysostom, *Homily 46 on Matthew 13: 24-30.*

[377] Pope John XXIII, *Pacem in Terris*, 36.

[378] catholiceducation.org/articles/history/world/wh0087.html

[379] *www.vatican.va/.../john_paul_ii/.../hf_jp-ii_exh_20030628_ecclesia-in-e...*

[380] op.cit.. Hutson, p. 60.

[381] Ibid, Hutson, p. 61.

[382] op.cit.. Maritain, *Scholasticism and Politics*, p. 215.

[383] Christopher Dawson, *Religion and the Rise of Western Culture*, Image, 1958, p. 18.

[384] *Gaudium et Spes,* Preface.

[385] op.cit.. Dawson, p. 14.

[386] The Official Anthem of the United States, "The Star Spangled Banner."